The Well Teacher

Finding energy, purpose and passion in your teaching career

Ben Levinson

BLOOMSBURY EDUCATION
LONDON OXFORD NEW YORK NEW DELHI SYDNEY

BLOOMSBURY EDUCATION
Bloomsbury Publishing Plc
50 Bedford Square, London WC1B 3DP, UK
Bloomsbury Publishing Ireland Limited
29 Earlsfort Terrace, Dublin 2, D02 AY28, Ireland

BLOOMSBURY, BLOOMSBURY EDUCATION and the
Diana logo are trademarks of Bloomsbury Publishing Plc

First published in Great Britain, 2026 by Bloomsbury Publishing Plc

This edition published in Great Britain, 2026 by Bloomsbury Publishing Plc

A catalogue record for this book is available from the British Library

ISBN: PB: 978-1-8019-9817-8; eBook: 978-1-8019-9818-5

2 4 6 8 10 9 7 5 3 1 (paperback)

Cover design by Sophie Gordon

Typeset by Lumina Datamatics Ltd

Printed and bound in Great Britain by TJ Books, Padstow, Cornwall

MIX
Paper | Supporting responsible forestry
FSC® C013056

To find out more about our authors and books visit www.bloomsbury.com
and sign up for our newsletters
For product safety related questions contact productsafety@bloomsbury.com

Contents

Foreword

I have been a teacher throughout my whole career. I started at a tough secondary school in Essex. That first year of teaching was, exactly as Ben describes, challenging, delightful and exhausting. There was never a single day when I felt bored, but there were certainly days that I dreaded.

Building relationships is a central part of a teacher's role. I joined a very experienced staff, who had found ways to survive within that community. There was no mentoring, no team teaching, no shared scheme of work or lesson resources. I worked in several different classrooms and felt from the beginning that I was on my own. Sink or swim. Thankfully, there were some Year 7 classes where I quickly established a bond. There was one class, however, that I only taught for the last forty minutes every Tuesday afternoon. The lesson was supposed to be silent reading, but this was a lively raucous class and by the end of the day the last thing they wanted to do was to read quietly. I tried everything with that group to survive. Some weeks were better than others but there was one particular girl, Geraldine, who always wanted to argue, never joined in happily, caused me to doubt whether teaching was the job for me. I was leaving at the end of the year, getting married and moving to Leicestershire. One day I encountered Geraldine in the corridor, *'I heard you're leaving Miss?'* she challenged. I told her where I was going and why. Surprisingly, she responded, *'Oh…but you're one of the good ones Miss!'*. On the last day of the term, she brought me a wedding present. I still have that glass dish, it means the world.

This book is packed with a passion for teaching. We know that the job can feel unbearable at times but in other moments it is such an affirming, amazing career. Thinking back over my many years in schools it is the relationships with children, students, colleagues and families that remain in my mind. We talk about making a difference and amongst all the busyness of school life it is the positive impact that we have that is the most important.

After many years working across all phases of education I left headship to become the founding CEO of the Chartered College of Teaching. Our role is to empower the profession, building teacher knowledge, efficacy and compassion. I warmly invite you to join our extensive community of teachers and educationalists all seeking to 'find a way through' within our amazing profession.

Dame Alison Peacock, DL, Chief Executive, Chartered College of Teaching

Introduction

Teaching is a wonderful job.
Teaching is an important job.
Teaching is a challenging job.
Teaching **should** be a job filled with joy.

This book sets out why teaching can be brilliant and gives you some practical tips about how you can make it work for you. (To be honest, in lots of this you could replace teaching for any other profession. But, also, some parts are uniquely teaching. Because it is a uniquely brilliant job.)

The fact is, teaching has the potential to be a positive force for your wellbeing. I know how that might sound to some people in the current context, but it is true. The component parts are all there:

- purpose
- relationships – with children, colleagues, families
- opportunities to learn every day.

I came into teaching – as so many people do – to make a difference. I also came into teaching because I wanted a job that I didn't just get through but flourished in. Work is such a big part of our lives, we should try and do something we genuinely love and are passionate about. It's not about minimising work, but rather maximising the joy and pleasure from work; the meaning and purpose; the positive impacts all of this has on your sense of self, self-confidence, self-esteem and wellbeing. Work-life integration rather than work-life balance. Of course, far too much work is absolutely not good for our wellbeing – we look at how to avoid burnout in Chapter 4. But it is more often work that is meaningless that can silently impact our health (BBC, 2021).

Have I always achieved this? No. But I have definitely learned a lot along the way and I hope that some of this will help you, wherever you are in your teaching journey.

Why work?

First, let's go back to the beginning. Why do we work?
It could be a number of reasons:

- money
- purpose
- making a difference
- our contribution to the human story.

It's probably a bit of all of these, weighted differently depending on your own values, background, situation etc. Some of us have dreamt of following a certain career from our earliest years and have inspirational origin stories. Others have fumbled around, uncertain of where to place their time and effort. Many will have just seemingly ended up doing what they do through a series of choices and coincidences that led them from school into work.

The last 50 years have been characterised by change. The world of work is no different. A 'job for life' is long gone. A 2021 Department for Education report showed that two-thirds of people had a portfolio career – one where you are working multiple roles concurrently – or looking to start one (People Management, 2021). A recent poll showed 25-34 year olds had already worked in six different roles (Fennell, 2025). This was particularly stark compared to people who were approaching retirement, who had only worked in seven. In The Future of Learning Global Report, a fifth of people said they expected to be working in a different industry within 10 years (Future Learn, 2022). And, of course, we know that a combination of automation and AI will dramatically change the work landscape in the coming years. McKinsey's report on this indicates potentially 400 million people having to change occupation as a result of these changes (Manyika et al., 2017). Helen Tupper and Sarah Ellis, founders of career development company, 'Amazing If', coined the term 'squiggly careers' for career paths that follow unconventional routes by taking skills and interests from both work and hobbies and applying them in different roles (Ellis and Tupper, 2020).

However you look at it, the fact is our working lives will look very different to those of our parents. Reflecting on why we do what we do will be crucial. In the 21st century we have an abundance of choice – just go to the supermarket to buy some tea for evidence of this. Sometimes that choice can be overwhelming (see the previous example) and we just want a standard cup of tea – I really do want a cup of tea now! Anyway, my point is that the changes and the choice allow us greater opportunity and flexibility. If you train to be a teacher you are not committing your whole life to it. If you are not a teacher now but are thinking about it, it's entirely possible to change.

Teaching is brilliant

If you've picked this book up, chances are you are a teacher or thinking about becoming one. I think it would also be a reasonable assumption that you've seen or heard some negative stories about teaching. Because – let's be honest – most of the stories in recent times have been negative.

And let's be clear from the outset, I am not here to tell you the system is all sunshine and rainbows. In fact, far from it. There are a lot of challenges. A whole heap of challenges. From funding to attendance to behaviour to special needs to accountability and more. And these challenges can create monsters of people, which leads to some less than desirable (at times frankly toxic) working environments in individual schools and across individual multi-academy trusts. But – and this is the big BUT – teaching is a brilliant job. Let me just say that again, louder for those of you at the back:

TEACHING IS A BRILLIANT JOB!

Because, when you boil it all down, it's you and 30 children and the opportunity to change their lives. And that's the point. You can properly change their lives, and you can see those changes happen in front of your very eyes. It's magical and, as we'll hear from teachers throughout this book, it is what makes teaching a job like no other. So, in a world of abundant choice, where you are likely to have multiple jobs in multiple industries, and it will all change in the next 20 years, I'm here to convince you that teaching should be at the top of your list when you're thinking about what to do. And if you are already teaching, I hope I can show you why you should continue and how you can do that whilst looking after yourself. Along the way, I will share advice from a whole range of teachers about what they do to make the job enjoyable and sustainable.

Circles of influence

In writing this book, I really wanted to offer something that helped you to take control of your wellbeing by focusing on what is within your direct circle of influence (those factors you have direct control over). I've already mentioned the education system and organisational challenges around wellbeing. More often than not, we have little or no control over these. So I want to be really clear:

> *I am not excusing or ignoring these.*

I am well aware they exist and can be powerful factors in your wellbeing. But this book is all about what you can do to support your wellbeing. It will empower you to make the changes you can make, affect what you can affect, and allow you to make the best of yourself and your current situation. After that, only you can decide if this is your lifelong dream or a step on your squiggly career path.

I hope that you both enjoy and take something of value from the following chapters. If it helps just one teacher, it will be worth it.

Dedication:

For Chloë, Eva, Noa and Esme – my daily reminder of what matters most.

Finding the magic

1 The spark

'The purpose of life is not to be happy. It is to be useful, to be honorable, to be compassionate, to have it make some difference that you have lived and lived well.'

Attributed to Ralph Waldo Emerson

'Finding your element is vital to understanding who you are and what you're capable of being and doing with your life'

(Robinson, 2014, p. xiii).

The first reason teaching can impact positively on your wellbeing is that it is a profession full of purpose. This is one of the key reasons it is such a wonderful career. That feeling of purpose is almost always every teacher's key reason – for starting to teach *and* for continuing.

Maybe you're reading this because you do love teaching and want to know how you can sustain it. Maybe you're reading it because you once loved teaching, but are now exhausted and want to be reminded why you started in the first place. Maybe you're starting to question if it is the right career for you. Or maybe you're considering it and trying to decide if becoming a teacher is the right path to take. Maybe you think you'd love it but you've heard lots of bad things?

This first chapter is about 'the spark' – that purpose that drives the profession. What ignites it, what dims it, and how you can tend it or reignite it. I start by taking you through my teaching journey in the hope that you can find parallels here for yourself, before exploring why finding and tending your spark is so important. Along the way, there'll be activities you can do to help develop your spark. We'll also take a look at what other teachers' sparks are to provide further inspiration.

From office to classroom: finding my spark

My mum was a teacher. I never knew what I wanted to do with my life. I did well at school and enjoyed it but I never had that dream. I didn't want to be an astronaut or a doctor. I didn't dream of becoming a lawyer or a footballer. I had a brief dalliance (in my mind at least) with playing rugby for England but I wasn't anywhere near good enough or hardworking enough to make that a reality. My mum's advice: do not go straight from education to education, experience the world outside school. So, being the good boy that I am, I listened to my mum and went out and got a job.

I landed a job in an IT company and fell into their marketing department. When they suggested I moved to their European office in Eindhoven I jumped at the chance. It was all good fun but, increasingly, I wanted to make a difference. I was trying to convince people to buy something that was the same (or worse) than the competitor's model – it didn't exactly inspire me to get out of bed every day. So I moved to an environmental charity. 'They're doing good in the world', I thought, 'that will scratch this itch.' And it did, for a while. But I was still sitting behind a desk. And, frankly, I was bored. I'd watch the clock. I'd count down the minutes to the weekend. I'd grasp on to every holiday like it was my last. I was bored. Perpetually bored.

Upon reflection, what those jobs taught me was that I needed my work to really mean something. It wasn't enough for it to be fun or well-paid or 'doing good' in a vague sense – I needed to see the *tangible* impact of what I was doing, to feel like I was really helping someone. That feeling led me to teaching, but it is also something I've carried with me throughout my time in education.

By now, I'd got together with Chloë – a teacher – and was spending lots of time with her colleagues. They were a great group and we naturally spent a lot of time talking about education. It was fascinating. They were so passionate about what they did. And they had so many stories about their days at work. Every day was different. They were making a real difference. It was so hands on, fast-paced and exciting. They had real connection: with the children, the families, and each other. I'd sit and listen to them discussing education, the children and families they were working with, and their hopes and dreams for the future. I couldn't help contrast it with my rather mundane office job, sitting behind a desk. It wasn't that they were endlessly positive about it – quite the opposite a lot of the time – but they did really care. You could see the fire, the excitement, the 'spark.' It wasn't long before I knew what I wanted to do.

♥ Well moment ♥

Write a message to your partner/friend/colleague, from the version of you who first chose this job. What mattered to you then? What still does? Use this to reconnect with your spark. Or if you're about to start out, do it now and keep it somewhere you can refer back to.

The early days: maximum spark

Of course, it turned out my mum had known all along I was going to follow this route (mums, they're just the best aren't they?!) I'd spent odd days, either when holidays overlapped or when I had a day off, going in to help out wherever mum was teaching. She'd taught in a couple of schools for disabled children and children with significant special educational needs. All of the children were in need of constant care and support, and some of the conditions were life-limiting. That was tough. Emotionally and physically. Some students were as old as 18 and physically very strong, which could be exceptionally challenging when they became dysregulated. But mum saw my love of the job and my passion for working with children straight away. I can't say I did at first, but I do have some great memories of helping out. I still remember many of the children's names, and I remember a sports day with them that was particularly joyful, seeing everyone full of life and laughter. I guess the spark found its way in on that day and waited for its chance to ignite.

I got a place on the Graduate Teacher Programme (GTP) and started my training. It was tough but I loved it: working with the children, building those relationships, seeing the difference I was making. And, I was *never* bored. No more looking at the clock. No more wishing the hours and days away. It was so varied. There were so many opportunities to take and so much to think about. I was working with a great group of people – both the team at the school and the other trainees. And of course, I was learning so much! It was non-stop. The intellectual challenge is the part I remember most from the beginning. So much to think about and understand in terms of pedagogy, child development, curriculum, behaviour, the list goes on. But I just loved it.

Most of all, I loved the sense of purpose. I'd never felt fulfilment like I did in that first year on the GTP. I'd literally bounce into school every day and be the first one there, waiting for the caretaker – Bambos – to open up. (Bambos was a diamond. A delightfully surly man with a heart of gold. In the end, I started knocking for him as I walked past his house and we'd go into school together.)

Reality bites and the spark flickers ever so slightly

Despite my love of the job, it was tough. I was working long hours and I was tired. The school was great but there was just so much to do. So much to think about in a lesson, in a day, a week, a term. There were simply so many elements that went into the job. It often felt overwhelming. Assessment for Learning (AfL), scaffolding, challenge, pace, learning objective, success criteria. Links to previous learning/future learning; starter, main, plenary; praise, sanctions, rewards;

questioning - cold calling, random selection, hands up? Support for children with special educational needs; challenges for Gifted and Talented children; subject knowledge; links to real world purpose; modelling; group work; circulating; feedback. Resources; use of technology; classroom layout; displays, engagement; independence, pupil voice; inclusion, addressing misconceptions… and that's only scratching the surface. How could one person ever hold this all in their head? How could you *ever* do this work intentionally, purposefully and meaningfully?

> **♥ Well moment ♥**
>
> **List three parts of your job that give you your 'spark' and three that deflate you. Can you spend more of your time on the first group and less (or none?) on the second?**

Overload: the spark becomes a glimmer

As I grew in experience, some of it became automatic. Much like driving a car; I no longer had to think every time I changed gear. But it was still tough. I changed schools after a few years. Then I got a role as deputy headteacher, and *then* the headteacher left at the end of my first term and I was asked to take over that role. The school 'required improvement' (and not just because Ofsted said so). And it continued to be tough. My first daughter – Eva – had been born a year into my teaching career, my second – Noa – a year before I took on the headship. So on top of everything else, I had a one year old and a three year old at home. To be honest, all of this nearly finished me off. I was working long hours and I was stressed. I was coming home to a young family. I had no time to myself. I started to get heart palpitations and migraines. Clearly, this wasn't sustainable.

According to the 2024 Teacher Wellbeing Index, around a third of teachers reported symptoms that suggested burnout (Education Support, 2024). This is a stark reminder that passion alone is not enough.

> **♥ Well moment ♥**
>
> **There is help out there. Education Support is an amazing organisation, supporting people working in schools. If you are finding it really hard, please speak to someone. Education Support's 24/7 helpline is one option: 08000 562 561.**

Burnout

Burnout isn't just 'being tired' – it's a state of chronic emotional, physical, and mental exhaustion caused by prolonged stress and overwork. The World Health Organization's International Classification of Diseases (ICD-11) defines burnout as, 'resulting from chronic workplace stress that has not been successfully managed,' (World Health Organization, 2024). In teachers, it can look like cynicism, detachment, a sense of ineffectiveness, or that feeling of dragging yourself through each day on autopilot. If that sounds familiar, you're not alone – and you're not broken. That spark hasn't gone out forever, but it might need some care to flicker back to life. When this happened to me, I didn't have the language for burnout, but that's exactly what this was. Teaching pushed me to the edge – emotionally, physically, mentally. I've since learned that if you want to do this work for life, you need to do it in a way that gives life back to you too.

♥ Well moment ♥

From burnout to balance

- Identify one boundary you can put in place this term.
- Reflect on whether your current pace at work and home is sustainable – if not, what could change?
- Talk to someone you trust about what keeps your spark alive.

Did I still love what I did? I still cared as deeply – maybe too deeply at times. I certainly wasn't bored. It meant something. I felt happy to be making a difference. There were many magical moments and memories amongst the challenges. Like the time we had a science fair and one of our amazing teachers – who was also a baker – created incredible themed cakes and biscuits: cupcakes with syringes filled with caramel to squirt into them; biscuits that looked like actual hearts; cakes filled with popping candy. I was still learning so much. I was working with some great people and meeting many more. But, I could not continue in this vein.

Tending the spark

I started to try and understand how to make it work. How I could manage the load and hold onto myself in all of this. (And, in doing, how everyone else could as well.) So began a journey of self-discovery and an understanding of health and wellbeing. Knowing myself. Knowing my limitations. Understanding that this was a marathon, not a sprint. That I wanted this to be my life's work. And, by making it my life's work, I would have far greater impact and make far more of a difference. I needed to keep that spark alive.

Fast forward to today and it is a very different picture. Part of that is due to experience but the greatest part was the realisation that to truly make a difference, I had to look after myself first and foremost. As I said at the outset, none of this is separate from the system changes that are needed. None of it will make you immune to a toxic environment. But, back to our circles of influence, it will empower you to make the changes you can realistically make, affect what you can affect, and allow you to make the best of yourself and your current situation. After that, only you can decide if this is your lifelong dream or a step on your squiggly career path. But if you can get it right, it can not only sustain you but can actually positively contribute to your wellbeing.

♥ Well moment ♥

Tending the spark – quick wins to try this week

- Revisit a favourite success story and write down what made it special.
- Do one thing that reminds you why you teach. Whether it's reading with a child, planning a creative activity, or taking a moment to really connect – seek out the bit that brings you real joy.
- Name your impact: at the end of one day this week, jot down a specific way you made a difference – however small.
- Ask a colleague: 'What's one thing that keeps you going in tough weeks?'

Why is finding and tending your teaching spark so important?

Why is that important? *Is* any of that important? Well, I think so. I think it is profoundly important. What separates humans from any other species is our ability to pass on knowledge, skills and ideas from generation to generation.

We are all standing on the shoulders of giants. In cultural anthropology this is known as the 'ratchet effect' – '...the point at which culturally transmitted information begins to accumulate over generations, such that tools and know-how get increasingly better fit to the local environments' (Henrich, 2017, pp. 56–57). So our collective future success and happiness depends on our ability to effectively educate the next generation.

As an act of altruism and as an attempt to improve the human condition, nothing holds more potential for change than teaching. Consider some worldwide issues that concern you. Climate change? Crime? Addiction? Poverty? Inequality? Technological advancement? War? Or closer to home. Littering? Dog mess? Antisocial behaviour? Whether global or local, teaching and education is one of the most powerful levers we have as a society to address big challenges and influence change. Whether you want to fundamentally change the world or just one life, teaching is the tool by which you can. If everyone was better informed and better educated, the world would be a better place. End of.

Teaching is also about hope. We have got ourselves into a negative space in general. Yes, about education and teaching but also about so much more. We live in the most abundant time in human history. It's not perfect but it is so much better in so many ways than 50/500/5,000/500,000 years ago. Max Roser's fantastic website, *Our World in Data* demonstrates this in multiple ways. For example, the percentage of people living in extreme poverty globally has dropped from 75 per cent in 1820 to 10 per cent in 2018 (Roser, 2019). Just 30 years ago it was over 30 per cent! As Hans Rosling demonstrates in *Factfulness*: 'Step-by-step, year-by-year, the world is improving' (Rosling, 2019, p. 13). To be a teacher is to have hope in the future and the potential of people - through education and learning - to continue to develop, improve and succeed.

Because it is education that drives this progress. The work teachers do collectively in empowering people to solve problems, challenge injustice, think creatively and collaborate is what leads to a better future. Your contribution as a teacher provides the opportunities for the next generation, creating a ripple effect that moves the human race ever forward.

What humans have achieved is astonishing. In this country right now, you can pick up a phone, click a few buttons and in the next 24 hours (or sooner) an abundance of food can arrive at your doorstep. This would have utterly astounded our ancestors. And what do we do? Moan about the fact it can't come quicker; that someone has thought it is appropriate to substitute apples with pears; that we have to put it all away - eugh, *so* boring! why haven't they invented a robot for this yet?! And that's just the tip of the iceberg. But education and teaching are about hope. They are about believing that we can be better. That the young people truly are our future.

To be a teacher is to be a believer. It is to believe that your investment will make a difference. That there is hope and that this species will endure, will find solutions, will grow and improve and continue on its astonishing journey. And so there is arguably nothing more important than having enough brilliant people who find and tend their spark to achieve all of this.

We started with teaching being a fantastic career that can impact positively on your wellbeing: nothing brings more meaning than teaching. When I spoke to the teachers whose case studies feature in this book, that was the greatest driver. Time and again I heard of the purpose that teaching brings. The difference you can make to the lives of so many people. Are there other careers that can give you this sense of purpose? Sure. A few. Obvious ones like doctors. Or politicians (no need for that laughter back there!) But so many of them add so little real value beyond fuelling the capitalist system we operate in. And, yes, in that capitalist system the taxes people pay fund the education system we have but, for many jobs, I'd argue that it's hard to find much value beyond that. Which is pretty depressing when you think about it. Getting up every day to make a difference and to believe in the potential of these incredible – at times challenging – young people… that sounds like a sure-fire way to keep your spark alive to me. And with that spark, comes that purpose.

If your spark has dimmed

You may not feel this spark right now. Maybe that's why you picked this book up. That's OK. You might feel burned out or angry. Too many people are. This chapter isn't about nostalgia. And – like every part of this book – none of it is a solution to all of the challenges we face. But by remembering what got you here and why it still matters, you can start to rebuild part of that purpose and meaning. In doing that, you can start to take back control, shape your own experience, and own the difference you make. I hope that is the first part of restoring joy, wellbeing and agency in your career.

Once you've found your spark, you need to nurture it and care for it. You need to invest in yourself and build your personal capital. You need to find ways to manage your load, keep growing, find the joy and positivity, and set the challenges alongside the bigger picture – the difference you are making to the lives of the young people you work with. The rest of this book will explore *how* to do this.

Here are the 'sparks' for some other people:

Stories from the classroom

Inspired by compassion

Harmeet always knew she wanted to be a teacher, but her spark grew stronger because of her experiences. As a teenager facing significant challenges at home – including a parent struggling with alcoholism – she found refuge in the kindness of two remarkable teachers. One of them, her form tutor, became a lifelong role model. 'She was the first person outside my family I ever told about my difficult home life,' Harmeet shared. That teacher didn't just listen, she gave Harmeet books, helped her apply to college, and even took her to see *Hamlet*, buying the ticket for her. This teacher supported Harmeet long after school ended and remained a guiding presence until her death. Now, Harmeet teaches with her in mind. 'I don't think I'm that selfless, but if I'm even half of what she was…' she said. That spark – the sense of being seen and supported – drives her to mentor new teachers and go the extra mile for students. For Harmeet, teaching is about passing on the lifeline that once saved her.

Harmeet, secondary school teacher

From gymnastics to the classroom

Sonya never planned to be a teacher. Her life was devoted to gymnastics: first as an athlete, then as a coach. She even ran a gym in Ireland with her sister. But when the business failed, Sonya found herself at a crossroads. A friend asked her to help at a summer camp for children with special educational needs and that experience shifted everything. 'I just fell in love with working with children,' she recalled. That led her to a job as a Teaching Assistant (TA), where she kept being told she should train as a teacher. At first, she laughed it off. She hadn't even been to university. But eventually, the pull became too strong. Ten years later, Sonya is now a computing specialist – a field she never imagined herself in. 'I love my job,' she told me. 'I come in every day smiling.' Her journey reflects a theme shared by many teachers: sometimes, the spark for teaching doesn't appear at the start, it's found in the *doing*.

Sonya, primary school teacher

A career reinvented

Chaz didn't start out in education. For over a decade, she built a career in brand marketing. Then life – and a transatlantic move – prompted a rethink. 'I'd had a good time,' she said of her previous role, 'but I was done.' Teaching had always been in the back of her mind, but her psychology degree wasn't considered a traditional route into the profession. Only when her circumstances changed did she find the space to pursue it. Now in her fourth year, Chaz speaks of her transition with clarity and pride. 'I don't think I wanted to do [marketing] for the next 30 years,' she said. The spark for teaching came not from a lifelong dream but from reflection, timing and a deep sense of wanting to do something that mattered. 'I've never looked back,' she said. Now she brings the insights from her previous career into every lesson.

Chaz, secondary school teacher

Well reflections

- What was your spark? Why did you first become a teacher?
- When did you last feel a strong sense of purpose?
- What keeps the spark alive for you now?

Well practice

(Re)connecting with your spark:

- What motivates you in life?
- What do you want/need from work?
- Reflect on this and identify your key motivations.
- Are/could you get these from teaching?
- Are there other careers that would give you these?
- Make a table listing the pros and cons of each of those careers that fulfil your key motivations.

If this helped you reconnect with your spark, the next step is learning how to carry that spark through the daily realities of the job – and that's exactly what we'll explore in the next chapter.

2 Joy, hope and positivity

'Whether you think you can or whether you think you can't, you're probably right.'

Attributed to Henry Ford

'He who fears he shall suffer already suffers what he fears'

(Michael Montaigne, 1685).

Teaching should be a profession typified by joy, hope and positivity. However, that is not the current narrative nor the experience of many teachers. The causes of this situation – government policies, curriculum and assessment strictures, funding, institutional cultures – are largely outside of a lone teacher's ability to influence. But that does not mean teaching is irreparably broken for the individual teacher. This chapter explores ways in which you can take back control and make your days, weeks and years more joyful, hopeful and positive. In so doing, you have an opportunity to positively impact your wellbeing because teaching offers more chances in a day for joy, hope and positivity than most careers do in a lifetime. And, as Martin Seligman describes in his book *Flourish*, 'Positive psychology makes people happier' (Seligman, 2011, p.2). Or as Barbara Fredrickson puts it, 'Positivity can uniquely revitalize your worldview, your mental energy, your relationships, and your potential' (Fredrickson, 2011, p.14).

Being aware of your negativity bias

The idea of 'negativity bias' was first coined in 2001 by psychologists Paul Rozin and Edward Royzman. It is a basic survival instinct – we are programmed to look out for negative information because it is more likely to indicate a threat to our safety (Rozin & Rozyman, 2001). If we are cold or sense danger, we need to respond to that more rapidly. Like so many of these instincts, they were hugely helpful through much of our evolution but less so today. Research in 2023 on media websites showed that, for a headline of average length, each additional negative word increased the click-through rate by 2.3 per cent (Robertson *et al*, 2023). One teacher told me, 'I am sometimes my own worst enemy in that I overthink everything. I think that's because I want to always be my best' (Daniella, primary school teacher).

Of course, this is not the same as saying there is nothing to be negative about. As I said at the start, the current system has many challenges (as does the modern classroom). So the question is not whether there is anything to be negative about – there are always reasons you could be negative – the question is what is the best way to help yourself? Will focusing on the negatives improve your situation? Will it help your wellbeing? Will it enable you to achieve what you want to achieve? In my experience, whilst briefly dipping your toe in the waters of negativity is fine – it can help you to identify where change is needed or find an alternate solution – the fact is, intentionally choosing joy, hope and positivity is one of the most effective ways to improve your wellbeing and move towards your goals.

♥ Well moment ♥

Create a personal 'joy menu'. Make a list of small, everyday things that bring you joy – a chat with a child, saying 'hi' to a colleague, seeing children focused on their learning.

The purpose of 'joy'

'The good life is joyful… and challenging. Full of love, but also pain'

(Waldinger and Schulz, 2025, p.3).

'...real toughness is experiencing discomfort or distress, leaning in, paying attention, and creating space to take thoughtful action [...] Toughness is navigating discomfort to make the best decision you can'

(Magness, 2022, p.13).

Now, just in case anyone thinks I'm being frivolous, I think it is important to note that resilience and wellbeing are fuelled by joy. I'm not talking about the manic, at-all-costs, painted on smile kind of joy. I'm talking about *genuine* joy. As Waldinger and Schulz (2025) emphasise, it is foundational to health and longevity. While Magness (2022) underlines that resilience requires attentiveness to what energises us and brings us positivity and joy.

Researchers in Brazil showed the link between laughter and improvements in heart health and circulation (Saffi *et al*, 2023). Genuine joy comes from positive relationships (more on this later) and interactions; achieving something of meaning, or experiencing a sense of awe or wonder. In the teaching profession, all of these are available in abundance.

Joy in the every day

What is the point of doing this job if not for the joy? Yes, this job is crucially important. Yes, we have a great responsibility. Yes, we are highly trained, skilled professionals and, no, that is not recognised enough. But come on, you work in a school filled with children! There are (or certainly should be) so many opportunities for genuine joy. Part of that is the more basic 'fun' or 'happiness' but there is also the deeper sense of joy achieved through deep, meaningful relationships (more on these in Chapter 3); achieving something worthwhile, or experiencing a sense of awe and wonder.

♥ Well moment ♥

Moments of joy

1. Grab a pad of sticky notes at the start of the day.
2. Each time something joyful happens, note it down. You can do this for yourself or you can share what you are doing with your children – they are bound to be curious.
3. Collect them all and, at the end of the day, stick them all up: on the wall, your whiteboard, the fridge.
4. Stand back and take a moment to reflect on everything joyful that has happened – in just one day.

I hope you can see how many potential opportunities there are in schools for joy. This is not some corporate, monotonous drone of a job. It's filled with energy, excitement, passion, purpose and, yes, joy! Because there's enough challenge, difficulty, stress, confrontation and pressure. You have to balance it with noticing those joyful moments. But if you can't see that right now, I feel you. It can be tough when you are burned out or overwhelmed. If this applies to you, I hope the next section can at least start to nudge you in the right direction.

Finding joy in the learning

I sometimes worry that, in our drive to improve and be better, we have lost the joy. The developments in pedagogy, cognitive science, school improvement and so much more, are undoubtedly great. We have a better informed approach to teaching and learning than we ever have. And, of course, there is great joy in learning *per se*. Making progress; knowing more and doing more; getting truly lost in your learning bubble. These are all sources of great joy.

But, at times, it can feel that the drive for ever greater efficiency and effectiveness in learning can come at the expense of the sheer enjoyment of working with children. And, like everything, it needs balance.

As a child, I remember Mr Tobias fondly because he'd have his guitar out every two minutes when I was in Year 4. How much I learned that year from an academic perspective is debatable. So, Mr Tobias may have been a step too far. But equally, we do not want to go too far in the other direction.

In an over-packed curriculum with high stakes accountability measures, we still need to create the time to have fun with the children. When it snows, make snowmen and throw snowballs. When it's hot, have a water fight. Take time to chat with a child about what they love, what makes them laugh, what they're passionate about. That connection can bring joy for you both, but it also supports the learning. Attachment theory shows us children who are more settled and more secure are more confident and more willing to take risks and push themselves to achieve (Bretherton, 1992). That moment of connection and joy can be the key that unlocks a child's academic progress.

Equally, intentionally planning for those moments of joy can be great for both your wellbeing and for your children's progress. When planning your lesson, ask yourself – 'Where is the joy in this lesson?' Trying to build in a moment of joy in each lesson (or just one lesson a day/week to begin with) will support both your wellbeing and the children's engagement in the learning. It's a win-win. Then there is just being aware of the moments of joy. As one of the teachers I spoke to told me: 'There will always be something in the lesson, something a student says or does, that makes me smile' (Adam, secondary school teacher).

Joy in the flow

One of the ways joy manifests so powerfully in teaching is through what Mihaly Csikszentmihalyi termed 'flow state' (1990). Csikszentmihalyi talks about having clear goals, getting immediate feedback, and having a balance between challenge and skill (1990). These are all present throughout a day's teaching and it is why so many teachers I spoke to told me they were 'never bored'. Like Amy who said, 'Give me the purpose and the joy and excitement of working with children. Give me the difference I'm making. Give me the fact that I am never bored. I never look at the clock. I'll take that any day over an office job.' Or Joe, 'In the last 12 years of my teaching I've never thought "is it home time yet?" or "what time of day is it?" or "this day's dragging." The weeks and months just fly by.'

In my previous jobs, I was bored. Time dragged. I watched the clock. But, in teaching, I am never bored. Time flies. There is never enough time! The limiting factor is always my physical and mental energy. So often, I am in a flow state: intensely focused; automatic in my actions; in control; enjoying the activity itself. This flow state is another element of deeper joy:

> *'...people are so involved in an activity that nothing else seems to matter; the experience itself is so enjoyable that people will do it even at great cost'*
>
> (Csikszentmihalyi, 1990, p.4).

Well practice: finding your flow

How can you find your flow? Consider the three elements Csikszentmihalyi talks about in his book, *Flow*:

- setting clear goals
- getting immediate feedback
- a balance between challenge and skill.

Carry out a quick self-assessment. Where do you sit against these three areas?

- **Clear goals:** are you clear what you want to achieve? In a lesson, day, week, term, year? Can you note down one thing you want to achieve at the start of each day?
- **Feedback:** there is no lack of this if you want it. How do children give feedback on your lessons? Can you end each lesson by asking them to make a note of what helped their learning the most and sticking it in their book?
- **Challenge and skill:** professional development is there in abundance in education. Chapter 6 explores the wellbeing benefits of continuing to grow professionally. How about setting yourself a target to learn something new each term? How do you want to do that? By reading an article? Talking to a colleague? Reflecting on your practice? If you keep it small and focused, you'll be amazed how quickly those build up and you can better match your skills to the challenges you face.

Hope and positivity through visualisation and manifestation

Both of the quotes at the start of this chapter have been close to my heart for many years now. Ford's attributed quote speaks so powerfully to the exceptional strength of the mind and of thought. It plays directly into the idea of visualisation, a technique used by many of the world's top sports people. Watch the athletes before the start of the 100m Olympic Final and you will see them staring down the track, visualising their perfect race. Legendary sprinter and long jumper Carl Lewis is commonly attributed as saying, 'Embrace the power of visualization and let your mind pave the path to victory.' That combination of hope and of positivity are such powerful bedfellows. Together they can pave the way to great achievements, and a far greater sense of personal wellbeing. Sir Tim Brighouse's famously attributed quote, 'The most important quality for anyone in education is unwarranted optimism,' continues to resonate strongly.

Of course, visualisation is a powerful tool in manifestation – the idea that you can turn your mental images into reality. Arguably, this is a more accurate description of what those 100m runners are doing – they are manifesting victory by *visualising* it.

Visualisation for manifestation

You may well be familiar with how to visualise through teaching children – particularly in reading. Visualisation for manifestation can be a great way to turn your hope into reality and make lessons run more smoothly, helping to boost your wellbeing.

Well practice

I find it helpful to:

- find a quiet space where I won't be disturbed
- close my eyes
- start by visualising what I want to do: clearly explain the learning, erudite questioning, moving learning forward, perfect balance of firm but friendly
- when I'm doing that, I will see: children happy, engaged, excited about their learning
- then take that into the other senses: what does that sound like?
- affirm it with a positive statement: this lesson is a great success; children have made excellent progress.

This can be helpful when you have the time but you can also do it in a quicker, simpler format:

Well moment version

Mid-lesson, step back and visualise your next interaction:

- What will you say?
- What will the response be?
- What will you see?
- Affirm: this is going to be an excellent interaction.

'But what if it *does* work out?'

I first came across this quote in Matt Haig's *The Comfort Book* (2021). Along with Montaine's (1685) words about suffering, it really hit home. I spent so much time with my head in the future – worrying about what might happen. All of that angst meant that, when it didn't happen – and invariably it didn't, I'd already lived all of the stress, worry and subsequent exhaustion as if it had gone catastrophically wrong!

I'll give an example. Each year we set off on our annual camping trip to Blackberry Wood in Sussex. It's one of my favourite parts of the year: the start of the summer holidays; a week with no phones or TV; set in beautiful English woodland, surrounded by nature and my favourite people (and our dog). Then that voice starts in my head: 'What if we don't fit everything in the car? What if our inflatable tent has a puncture? What if we don't get the pitch we asked for? What if there are noisy people next to us? What if the car breaks down?' And by the time we get there, all these 'what ifs' leave me exhausted and stressed. And, guess what? We *always* fit everything in the car, there's *never* been a puncture in the tent, we always get our pitch, everyone there is lovely and the car never breaks down. Will one of those things happen at some point? Probably. Will worrying about it have benefited me when it does? No.

We can see this happening in the classroom so often. 'What if Lewis has a bad day? What if my interactive whiteboard stops working when the headteacher walks in? What if the packed lunches aren't ready for our educational visit? What if…?' Finding ways to be hopeful and positive about the present and the future can dramatically shift your mindset and your daily experience. Or, as one of the teachers I spoke to said: 'But what if it does work out? What if you do have a great day?' (Daniella, primary school teacher).

Hope and positivity aren't just helpful when it comes to wellbeing; they are essential for life and for being a successful, sustainable teacher. Finding hope and positivity gives you the tools you need to navigate the unpredictable, chaotic nature of working with children and young people in all their wonderful, crazy variety. They can help you to keep going, keep believing, and keep bringing energy into the classroom.

♥ Well moment ♥

Shifting your mindset to one of hope and positivity can happen in a moment but – like anything – it takes practice to shift it permanently. Here's a list of quick activities you can try that. If they're done regularly, they might help you make that change.

Reframing

Catch your negative self talk and reframe it. Rather than, 'what if it goes wrong?' reframe it as, 'what if it goes right?' Use your visualisation to really imagine it going brilliantly.

Positive journaling

Take 10 minutes each day to write about one small aspect of your life and how it would look if it was going as well as it possibly could. 'The children line up as soon as I ask them. I share a joke with Rameesha. They file out beautifully. Leo pulls me to one side and says, "I'm really enjoying science since I came into your class".'

Small wins

Try and start each lesson with a small win. Whether it's an interaction or an activity, engineering success early on will build both your confidence and your children's.

Finishing strong

At the end of the day, note down what went well rather than ruminating on what didn't.

Joy, hope and positivity: putting on your rose-tinted glasses

It was a Tuesday; around 12.15 pm. I was on duty in the dinner hall. I'd had a reasonably stressful morning. Nothing out of the ordinary but I could feel my shoulders were a couple of inches higher than usual – a sure sign. I was tired: a significant trigger of stress for me. And I was hungry: my other main trigger. I was doing what I'd done ever since my very first playground duty… looking for the warning signs of 'trouble'.

I take pride in being able to pre-empt issues. I am extremely vigilant and I've always 'walked towards the noise'. As I stood there, I noticed some children standing up, so I went to ask them to sit down: the shoulders went higher. A couple of children shouting to each other: higher.

I could feel my calm outer persona beginning to crumble. I knew that unless I did something, I was going to erupt – and then regret it. I knew I'd regret it because, not only would I let myself down by not effectively managing my emotions, but that level of emotional dysregulation would also stay with me for the rest of the day, perhaps even into the next day. At that point, I remembered what we'd been discussing in a staff meeting the previous evening. We'd spent the autumn term looking at the children who were working towards age expected. That Monday evening, we discussed looking at them in different ways, using the six lenses set out in *Look*. One of them was 'rose-tinted glasses' – looking at the positive aspects only (Pine II & Gilmore, 2006).

I stopped looking for where things were going wrong in that moment and started looking for where it was going right. The children sat beautifully eating their food: my shoulders relaxed lower. The children laughing with a colleague: lower. Our lunchtime leaders helping the younger children with their water: lower. A child asking for help opening their crackers, with impeccable manners and not needing to be reminded: lower. It was a beautiful experience and truly transformational. In a couple of minutes, I'd gone from simmering to relaxed. I could physically and mentally feel the difference.

That rose-tinted lense moment taught me the power of choosing joy, hope and positivity. By focusing on what was good I completely shifted my perspective and my mindset. I reduced my stress and became a calmer, more energised version of myself. Now I try to do that regularly and really take the time to focus on what is working, not on what isn't. Once you start to build this habit, it can transform both your approach and your wellbeing.

Well practice: shifting your perspective

It sounds so simple – just look for the positives! But we know that it's not. Here's how to do it:

1. **Catch your thoughts:** being self-aware and identifying when you are thinking negatively is the first step. What's your internal dialogue? Are you focusing on the negative?
2. **Reframe those thoughts:** from 'that child can't' to 'that's useful information – how can I help?'
3. **Direct your attention:** attention is a spotlight and you can point it at the negative interpretation or the positive one.
4. **Harness the power of curiosity:** all information is just that – information. Rather than putting a value judgement on it – good/bad; right/wrong – be curious. 'I wonder why…?'; 'What's that telling me…?'; 'How could I use that information…?'

Not only are we programmed to look for the negative as human beings, we double-down on that in schools. We are programmed to look for the 'bad'. What's going wrong? Where do we need to improve? What could be 'even better if'? We spend a disproportionate amount of time focusing on the children who 'aren't getting it.' Often we feel a lesson was a 'disaster' based on one or two children who didn't grasp the concept. Our AfL is skewed by the one child who *didn't* rather than the 29 that *did*.

(I often directed a question at the child I didn't think had got it – that was good assessment, right? However, when they verified my hypothesis, I allowed it to cloud my judgement: none of them understood; something is going wrong; disaster!)

There are good reasons for this. Our jobs are based on making improvements. We need to make sure we know who hasn't understood so that we can help them. However, sometimes this can be a) all-consuming and b) counter-productive.

Spending some time wearing your rose-tinted glasses is a great way to shift this mindset. Whether in your classroom or around the school, so much of what is happening is amazing. Children are learning, behaving beautifully and generally being incredible human beings. So much is happening that would make you incredibly proud. The challenge is to direct your attention towards it. I implore you to regularly spend a day, an hour, or even just five minutes, looking at the world from a different perspective. It will make you feel better, give you true perspective and help reduce your stress.

Taking the time to notice and create moments of joy; focusing on the positives, and thinking about what could happen if everything *does* work out, are all exceptional ways to improve your personal wellbeing. As we said at the start, there are few if any professions that provide you with the wealth of opportunities for joy, positivity and hope.

I want to be really clear, this is not about burying your head in the sand or ignoring the challenges. It's not pretending that everything is perfect and nothing needs to change. It is about making positive choices, that are within your circle of influence, which can make the difference. In doing so, you will also massively shift perspective on your agency. If you choose to be joyful, positive and hopeful, no one can take that away from you.

Well moments: tools for rebalancing

There will always be days when finding joy feels like an uphill climb. That's completely normal and it's exactly when intentional strategies can be most powerful. These small, structured tools can help re-centre your perspective and support your wellbeing:

Three wins journal

Each Friday, note three small wins from the week. They could be a moment of connection, something funny or interesting a child said, a breakthrough with a pupil or colleague, or simply dealing with a challenging situation well. Over time, you will build up a bank of positivity you can return to when things feel tough.

Positive sticky note

Keep a sticky note somewhere visible, (e.g. desk, diary, whiteboard) and update it daily or weekly with one moment that made you smile. It's a visual cue that joy is still present – even on the hardest days.

Joy buddy

Pair up with a colleague and share one highlight each week. Not only will it help you to identify the positive moment but it will also help in building connection – the theme of our next chapter.

Everyone will have their own stories of joy, hope and positivity. These are a few that were shared with me…

Stories from the classroom

Finding joy in the curriculum

Nuren teaches computing and STEM in a way that most schools hadn't seen before. When she started, she found the official computing curriculum nearly 12 years out of date – practically ancient history in tech terms. Rather than stick to it, Nuren reframed this as an opportunity to innovate. Every year, she overhauls her curriculum to include the latest developments, from simple robotics for little ones to AI-assisted coding projects for older pupils. This freedom to create keeps her and her students energised. In one project, her class of eight year olds used tablet apps to design their own video games, far exceeding the curriculum's old requirement of just learning keyboard skills. 'I love being part of what the future is going to create,' Nuren told me with a grin. As a result, her classroom buzzes with excitement – children as young as five dabble in programming robots, while older students discuss ethical hacking and machine learning. Nuren's creativity and focus on what she loves has brought real joy to both the children's learning and her job.

Nuren, STEM & computing specialist

The turnaround

Nate recently celebrated a particularly rewarding student success that encapsulates why he loves teaching. At his department's end-of-year awards evening, Nate honoured one of his A level economics students as Student of the Year – not for top grades, but for extraordinary growth and perseverance. This student started out as a quiet individual who had to work harder than his peers for average marks. But over two years, Nate watched him transform: he fell in love with economics, stayed late after school to improve, and even pursued a competitive business apprenticeship alongside his studies. Despite some early rejections, he kept trying. In the end, this student earned two coveted apprenticeship offers and dramatically boosted his exam performance.

The time invested in this young person and the difference it made is what brings Nate such deep joy and satisfaction in his role. Seeing the student stand up proudly to receive his award – and seeing the parents beaming with pride – was a high point of Nate's career. Moments like this, where you have worked hard and made a difference, remind Nate of why he does the job.

Nate, secondary school teacher

The pass that meant everything

For Devon, a secondary English teacher, one of the most uplifting moments in her career came on a nerve-racking exam results day. Devon had been tutoring a boy who was in danger of failing English – a student who often seemed to have given up on himself. Devon gave up lunch hours to run extra study sessions for him, sometimes scolding him gently for arriving late and reminding him, 'I'm giving my time to help you; you need to put in the effort too.' Slowly, the message got through. By the time exams arrived, the student was trying his best, even if his confidence was shaky.

When results day finally came, he had passed English. Devon will never forget the sight of the student sprinting over to her, eyes shining, to show off the passing grade. In that instant Devon thought 'I've actually done something good here.' The student thanked her, knowing Devon never gave up on him. Moments like that fuel Devon's hope – proof that with support and belief, even a struggling child can turn a corner.

Devon, secondary school teacher

Well reflections

- When do you feel most energised in the classroom?
- How might you intentionally create joy, rather than wait for it?
- How often do you use positive, hopeful language during a day? With others? With yourself?

3 The power of relationships

'...people who are more connected... are happier and physically healthier'

(Waldinger and Schulz, 2025, p.21).

'To feel a sense of belonging is to feel accepted'

(Eastwood, 2022, p.22).

Relationships are the foundation of positive wellbeing. They are also at the very heart of teaching. Every day, we navigate a complex web of human connection – with children, colleagues, parents, and leaders. The quality and success of these relationships shapes everything, from children's academic progress to how sustainable the job is. They can bring joy, meaning and purpose; stress, anxiety and difficulty. But above all, relationships are central to our wellbeing. What other profession places relationships so squarely at the heart of the work?

That's why it's worth pausing for a moment to really think about our relationships. Teaching provides so many incredible opportunities for connecting with people and building strong, lasting bonds. Yet another way the teaching profession has the potential to positively impact our wellbeing.

'The good life'

The importance of relationships for our wellbeing isn't just a warm, fuzzy idea – it's one of the most robust findings in psychological research. *The Harvard Study of Adult Development* is one of the world's longest running longitudinal studies. Having started 80 years ago, it has followed a group of men, their children and now their grandchildren. It has generated a vast amount of data and some incredible insights into what makes for a *Good Life* (the title of the book written by the study's current directors). And what is the conclusion? Well, what matters above all else for a long, happy, healthy life is... the power of our relationships. In Robert Waldinger's TED talk on the study he says, 'The people who were the most satisfied in their relationships at age 50 were the healthiest at age 80' (Waldinger, 2015).

Owen Eastwood's (2022) book *Belonging* builds on this, demonstrating the central role that a sense of belonging, and the relationships that create it, play in our health and wellbeing. The sense of trust and safety found in belonging allows us to excel at what we do. Belonging also reduces anxiety and stress. And this all stems from not only the relationships we form, but also the sense of being part of something bigger than ourselves.

The *Gallup 12* poll – which has been used across over 100,000 workplaces – measures employee engagement. Of the 12 statements, the one that stands out is: 'I have a best friend at work.' It may seem a little incongruous – 'We're not here to make friends, we're here to do a job!' I hear you cry – but nearly half of those who answer yes to this question would also recommend their organisation as a good place to work, versus 20 per cent who answered no. It would seem that having close friends is fundamentally important at work as well as in life.

Relationships with colleagues

Colleagues can be great for creating a sense of camaraderie. They can help transform a potentially lonely job into a fun and connected one. Your colleagues can be a fantastic sounding board and a way to elevate your practice through collaboration. So what do work relationships look like and how can you cultivate yours?

Making a (work) best friend

Maybe those two things are not as separate as we sometimes frame them. In terms of friendships, I think education is already way ahead of the curve. Maybe it's the intense nature of the job. Maybe it's the shared passion. Maybe it is just the type of people who are likely to choose teaching as a career. Whatever it is, unbreakable bonds are often formed. My mother-in-law has been retired for over 15 years and left her job as a headteacher 25 years ago. Yet, she still regularly goes on holiday with former colleagues and school governors.

I have found it is often when you go through challenges you form the strongest bonds - spirit of the blitz. I formed a really strong bond with my partner teacher when I was working at a school that I found particularly challenging. Their support each morning, just to chat through the day and to share our frustrations, and again after school, was invaluable.

But it's hardly surprising. According to 'Our World in Data', 2024, during our working lives we spend nearly 5 times as long each year with co-workers than we do friends (1,032 hours versus 255 hours). And over 2.5 times as long as we do with family (400 hours). In fact, the amount of time we spend with co-workers is almost on a par with the time we spend with our partner (1,084 hours). This is why having a work best friend is so important and having positive relationships with colleagues makes such a difference to our wellbeing.

Well practice: building connection

Maybe you find it easy to make friends, but maybe you don't. Maybe you did when you were younger but it's become harder as an adult. Here are a few thoughts and suggestions to help you. These are applicable whether you are new in a school or you've been there a while but your relationships have dwindled.

1. **Invest:** We sometimes forget how much time and energy we've invested to build our most meaningful relationships. Yes, sometimes we 'just click' with someone, but trust and connection take time. You need to show up consistently. When do you have a chance to connect with someone? Can you find more ways? Can you make five connections with them this week?
2. **Listen**: People want to be heard. It's hard in a hectic school environment to really listen. Active listening enables you to focus: maintain eye contact; really tune into what they are saying and how they are saying it, tune out other distractions; do not think about your response or what you think, just listen to what they are saying; empathise – why do they think/feel the way they do?
3. **Appreciate:** Everyone likes to be appreciated. It needs to be genuine but people are doing great things every day in schools. Notice it and name it to the person. Tell them they are appreciated and doing a good job.

The importance of genuine connection

In order to build real, meaningful connections, we often need to first understand ourselves. But in my case, knowing myself led to a reduction of what I needed most – strong connections with people. It was sharing who I *really* was that allowed me to build the deepest connections.

I read Susan Cain's treatise on introversion about 10 years ago. *Quiet* fundamentally dissects the extrovert world we live in and makes the case for the positivity of introversion as a way of being (Cain, 2012). It changed my life at the time. I had spent my whole life believing I was an extrovert. I had a great group of friends who I loved going out with. I was (and still am) extremely competitive and, let's be honest – and as Cain argues – being an extrovert is winning in Western society. So I had to have lots of friends, I had to be popular, I had to be fun and loud and out there, because that's how you 'won' at life. (A slight aside here. I was perpetually frustrated that whenever there was a big night out with a big group of friends, I would almost invariably get a headache or a stomach upset literally just before we were due to leave. It never occurred to me that this was anxiety about socialising in large groups. The innocence of youth!)

Through better understanding myself – and in this case, my more introverted nature – came a freedom. I felt validated to make positive choices about how and when I connected with people.

Introversion and teaching

Of course, if you do happen to be more of an introvert, schools are not necessarily set up for you! The constant social interaction and the busy, noisy environments can be overwhelming – for children and adults. Some people love the staff room at lunchtime but I know many who want to find a quiet space and just recharge in that time. Both options are OK. The same goes for evenings and weekends. When you've spent all day being 'on' socially you may just want to carve out solitary activities – or at least take time to decompress. As Dora, one of the teachers I spoke to, said: 'I had this meeting with you, and I wanted to fit in the gym, because I'm doing physio exercises to get stronger… I'll go to the gym and then the spa after for a steam. That's hugely helpful to pour out stuff from my cup.' Even minor tweaks to our decision making – and most of all giving ourselves permission – can make all the difference.

I realise now that I do need relationships. We all do. Investing time and care in them is so important.

Trust + Time + Vulnerability = Strong relationships

What I needed – what I'd argue we all need – is to have that connection on our own terms. For me that was building in time to recharge, having more one-on-one or small group time, and socialising for shorter periods of time.

Over time, I came to realise that understanding myself better was crucial. Giving myself permission to make choices on what I *wanted* rather than what I thought was expected of me was also fundamental. But what was of far greater value was understanding myself and then sharing this with the people in my life. Sharing my vulnerability; being open and honest. Once I started to do this, my bonds became stronger, my relationships improved and I could make more genuine connections.

> **Well moment**
>
> **Building deep, meaningful relationships requires us to be vulnerable. Find an opportunity to open up to someone. Start small with something that you found difficult or struggled with this week. See how it feels and what response you get. The more you can share your vulnerability, the more people will open up to you and the more you can build true relationships that go beyond the surface.**

Those relationships and that sense of belonging are crucial for us but they are also crucial for the children we work with. As UK Secretary of State for Education, Bridget Phillipson (2024) said, 'Every child should go to a school where they are free to be themselves, free to make friends, free to explore their talents. A happy, healthy child who knows, that deep down inside, they belong.' As with everything else, we can only support the young people we work with if we first invest in ourselves and build strong relationships. By showing how these steps allow us to thrive and be safe and secure, we can better support our students by modelling how they can apply this to their own lives.

Relationships with children

The relationships we build with the children are so central to the job. It is often these relationships that create the greatest joy, are the greatest driver for our purpose, and make the greatest difference. Our purpose at Kensington Primary School is: 'To build the relationships that allow our children to be happy and healthy and love learning.'

Education is a relationship business. It is all about how we connect with the children and how the children connect with us. I still remember my NQT (Newly Qualified Teacher) class so well. I really connected with them, and they responded so well as a result. They were confident and positive. I could really push them in their learning and they would rise to the challenge. We had great fun, but they also knew when to get their heads down and do the work. Your first class is always special but there are so many more children who I remember. I've been at Kensington Primary School for 12 years now and we have older siblings coming back for work experience. There's a special bond with some of those children. Although, as our assistant headteacher David said during staff briefing recently, it becomes alarming when we realise that we have not only taught our work experience cohort in the past, but their parents too! (I said that it would be time to call it a day when that became *grandparents*…)

These connections and relationships are at the heart of the job. There is hardly a celebrity interview that doesn't mention 'that teacher': the one who made all the difference. The most famous, of course, is footballer, Ian Wright's (2020) encounter with Mr Pigden, the teacher who he credited with giving him direction when he was going through a challenging time. Wright thought that Mr Pigden had died – he'd tried to track him down but to no avail – but they were then emotionally reunited in 2010.

All of the teachers I spoke to cited the relationships they have with the children as a key part of their job and a positive contributor to their wellbeing. As Dora told me: 'The connection that you get between people when they can see you're excited, and then *they* get excited, and you get excited because they're excited… that's what I really like.' Or Francesca, 'The joy you see in their eyes when you make that connection... when they finally grasp it, that makes it all worthwhile.' Or Joe, 'You've got 30 children. You are their class teacher. You're such a big part of 30 children's lives at one given time. It's quite a special thing, really.'

The most often quoted piece of advice from all these teachers was about 'being human'. It seems almost laughably naïve, but it comes back to the point in Chapter 2 about losing sight of the joy in teaching because of the drive to improve outcomes. I think the narratives around young people, the undoubtedly challenging behaviour that teachers have to deal with at times, and the way schools are structured can all create tension and even a sense of 'them and us'. Those teachers I spoke to had created the time and space to connect with the children as human beings first. Little things like finding time to chat about the weekend or their favourite football teams. Finding moments of empathy, to check in and show genuine compassion. Adam said to me: 'It's knowing that student. If they like going to the cinema, asking them what they saw at the weekend. Just having that interest in them gives you half a chance. Even if they don't like your subject, they'll respect you more and want to do the lesson.'

♥ Well moment ♥

Take 30 seconds to connect with a child in your class this week. What did they do at the weekend? What team do they support? What's their favourite sport/animal/music/food? Where did they last go on holiday?

The happy classroom

Of course, it is also important for your wellbeing that children's relationships with each other are strong. There is some great guidance in Adrian Bethune's, *Wellbeing in the Primary Classroom* on this, including his work on building 'tribal classrooms' (Bethune, 2018). At Kensington Primary School we have developed a 'Relationships and Regulation' policy, which supports our children in learning the skills and knowledge they need for building effective relationships. Just as it was for me, a crucial part of this is developing self-knowledge. Children need to understand their emotions and what it is they find harder to manage. They need to know when they need to change their situation and what they can do when they identify this. They also need to build empathy and understanding of others. Our bespoke Emotional Health curriculum complements the 'Relationships and Regulation' policy. All of this means the children have positive relationships, which reduces conflict, and improves teacher wellbeing.

You may not have a bespoke curriculum in your school that supports this. However, building connections with children; empathising with how they are feeling; understanding and being interested in what motivates them, and showing them that you really care, will all support their emotional growth and development. You may not be able to transform your relationship overnight – particularly not if you only see them once a fortnight – but you will start to create a connection. So often – particularly for our most vulnerable children – it is these moments of connection that are truly transformative. And if you can bring that connection through a moment of warmth and care, that will also reflect back onto you and your wellbeing. Fundamentally, we are all here to make that difference to children's lives.

Ultimately, relationships are a key component of our wellbeing as a teacher. Colleagues aren't just for Christmas… If you can find a best friend at work, if you can build those connections with colleagues and children (and parents), if you can bring your authentic self, and share your thoughts openly, you will have a foundation upon which you can both weather the storms and find the joy, hope and positivity we discussed in the previous chapter. All those moments that we love, that fill our hearts and make us cry with laughter, are only special because we share them with someone.

Stories from the classroom

Held up by colleagues

For Kristy, teaching has brought incredible highs and some difficult lows. A few years into her career, she hit what she describes as a 'breaking point'. 'Everything came crashing down,' she said. What pulled her back wasn't a formal support system or policy, but her colleagues. 'The relationships I had – the women I worked with, and my line manager, Kerry, – helped drag me back from a really dark place.' Those personal connections were a lifeline, providing emotional safety. 'It's not always about being professional. It's about human connection and you build it by being real with people.' Relationships with colleagues are central to Kristy's wellbeing and staying power in the profession. 'It's like a home,' she said. 'If it weren't for those relationships at that crucial moment, I don't think I'd still be in teaching.'

Kristy, primary school teacher

Teaching where it matters most

Gary teaches in North Manchester, where he grew up. His experience of school wasn't easy, but one teacher changed everything. 'My English teacher had the willingness to try and keep me focused. Without her, I wouldn't be in this meeting right now.' That spark stayed with him, guiding him into the teaching profession. For nearly 20 years, he's worked in the community he was raised in. 'It sounds cheesy but this is my way of giving back… giving my community the chance to thrive.' Teaching for Gary is a mission rooted in shared experience and deep empathy. He felt seen by a teacher, and then became that person for someone else.

Gary, secondary school teacher

Well reflections

- How can you make time and space to connect with the children you teach?
- We are all natural storytellers, this is a great asset. But we also spend a lot of time telling ourselves stories. We all too readily concoct a narrative. 'He doesn't like me.'; 'They're angry with me.'; 'She thinks I'm stupid/lazy/no good.' What story are you telling yourself right now? Can you reframe that? What hard evidence do you have for your interpretation? Is there a chance your interpretation is inaccurate? What if they actually thought something different?
- What can you do to better understand yourself?

4 Managing the load *From chaos to clarity*

'...the problem with trying to make time for everything that feels important... is that you definitely never will'

(Burkeman, 2022, p.41).

'When everything is a priority, nothing is a priority'

(Martin, 2012).

Like anything of real value, teaching takes hard work. Making that manageable is essential if you are going to thrive in the job.

The big lie

I remember being a newly qualified teacher and sitting down with a blank timetable to plan out what I was going to teach and when: Five hours of English, five hours of maths, 30 minutes guided reading every day. Two hours of PE, two hours of science, handwriting, spellings. By the time I got to history, geography, art and DT, I had one box left. How was I supposed to make this work?

The idea that any teacher (or any school for that matter) 'does it all' is simply a great, big lie. Schools cannot be all things to all people. Neither can teachers. At worst, you are dragged from pillar to post. Most of the time, prioritisation happens as a result of dogma and concerns about, 'what Ofsted wants'. To really get the best out of yourself for the children, prioritisation needs to be clear and considered.

So, what do teachers need to think about or do in a day? Let us begin...

Before school (and on the way in):

- remember your lunch, keys and lanyard
- worry about your own children and their childcare
- check for any urgent emails
- photocopy resources (the copier is jammed, again)

- quick chat with Pastoral Lead about an ongoing issue with a child in your form
- log on to your computer (it's not working)
- prep resources for the lesson you didn't finish yesterday
- update the date and learning objective on the board
- brief the cover teacher for a colleague who is off sick
- follow-up on a safeguarding disclosure
- track down a child you've been asked to 'keep an eye on'.

And now the day starts...

During lessons:

- calm a child in tears over their forgotten homework
- spot and record signs of potential safeguarding concerns
- adapt the task for at least six different learners
- deliver engaging, evidence-informed teaching
- handle a pupil storming out mid-lesson
- keep tabs on three simultaneous conversations and still explain long division
- handle low-level disruption: fidgeting, whispering, wandering
- reinforce behaviour plan for a specific pupil
- be simultaneously: inspiring, strict, fun, calm, fair and firm.

It's 10.30 am – and time for a sleep?
No, it's time for break duty!

Breaktime:

- supervise playground duty (whilst trying to eat a banana)
- break up an argument on the field
- patch up a grazed knee
- speak briefly to the SENDCo
- respond to 'Have you got 2 mins?'
- check emails for any urgent updates

- calm a pupil inside who can't cope with the playground
- manage a line of kids "just wanting to tell you something"
- reheat coffee from this morning (for the third time).

Admin, planning and paperwork:

- submit assessment data for three subjects
- upload work to online platforms for absent pupils
- write individual feedback for 60 books
- complete EHCP feedback form
- plan and resource next week's lessons
- prepare slides for the next Continuing Professional Development (CPD) session you're leading
- send in trip permission slips and risk assessment
- print and laminate resources for your intervention group
- respond to 8 emails marked 'URGENT'
- chase up a reply from the site manager, again
- record safeguarding concerns on CPOMS
- do performance management paperwork.

Behaviour and pastoral:

- log three detentions and phone two parents
- implement individual behaviour plans
- keep Child X inside at breaktime (again)
- reassure a child struggling with anxiety
- comfort a child crying about home issues
- liaise with DSL about disclosure made mid-lesson
- supervise a student who was removed from another class.

Lunchtime:

- attend a meeting you forgot you had
- supervise indoor play due to rain

- deal with sick child waiting in your classroom
- retrieve a class set of clipboards from a distant cupboard
- sneak in 10 minutes of marking
- reprint a worksheet a child left on the bus
- squeeze in a wellbeing check on a colleague
- pick up lunch and eat it standing up at the photocopier.

Mental load:

- remind yourself to submit trip paperwork
- worry about the parent you forgot to email back
- replay a behaviour incident, wondering what you missed
- think about your own kids and how you'll collect them from after school club
- wonder if you remembered to set the homework
- feel behind on absolutely everything
- try not to take a rude comment from a child personally
- wonder whether you're burning out
- stress about the upcoming parents' evening
- question your career (life?) choices (briefly)
- feel immense pride when a struggling child finally gets it
- beat yourself up for not being more patient
- remind yourself you love this job.

Swallow frustration when your friend moans about childcare and tells you how good you've got it because 'you get great holidays' (even though they 'work' from home four days a week!)

After school:

- supervise club/intervention/detention
- attend a CP meeting
- debrief with a colleague about a tricky incident
- mark 60 books with detailed feedback
- call three more parents

- support a child in tears at pick-up
- write up meeting notes or CPOMS logs
- update classroom displays before the Ofsted 'window' opens
- leave later than you meant to (again).

At home:

- remember the one resource you left on your kitchen table
- read your children a bedtime story
- answer a parent message that came in at 8.00 pm
- finish marking
- eat dinner while half-reading an education blog
- try to unwind but can't stop worrying about Child X
- fall asleep thinking about laminating.

Yes, I have exaggerated for effect. But I bet it resonated with you. It's a tough job. There is a lot to do. Far too much to do. As one of the teachers I spoke to put it: 'It was like trying to drink from a firehose in my first term' (Joe, primary school teacher).

> **♥ Well moment ♥**
>
> **The rule of three**
>
> **Start each day by listing three things you are going to do. Everything else is a bonus.**

We've already looked at the dangers of being bored at work. We've looked at the joy, hope and positivity we can gain from the job and what a difference this makes to our overall wellbeing. Doing the job well is what makes it interesting, engaging and purposeful. In turn, spending our time in ways that are interesting, engaging and purposeful is very important for our wellbeing.

The two crucial elements for me are:

1. Managing the load, or deciding what matters and letting the rest burn.
2. Making the load meaningful – it is not 'work' that is the problem, it is the type of work.

Decide what matters, then let the rest burn

This is likely to be one area where a significant amount of your agency is dictated by the school you work at. For some people, they will have very limited opportunity to decide what matters and what burns. Others will have a great deal of freedom. The *Serenity Prayer* teaches us:

> *'God, grant me the serenity to accept the things I cannot change,*
> *Courage to change the things I can,*
> *And wisdom to know the difference*
>
> (Niebuhr, 1951).

I'd say that's a good starting point. You will always have *some* agency. Once you've identified what it is you can change, you need to start making decisions. (Spend more time making this resource better or the flipchart? Chat to my colleague or make a cup of tea? Change the display or go home? Follow up on the safeguarding concern or phone the parent back?) You will make thousands of choices about your time each day. Many of these have to be fast tracked otherwise you'd never be able to manage the mental load. Apparently, Barack Obama wore the same suit every day. Not because he necessarily loved it – although I'm guessing he did – but because it meant he didn't have to *think* about it. By eliminating that decision – along with many others – he freed up mental capacity to focus on the decisions that mattered.

As teachers, we know all too well about 'cognitive load theory' – the theory that our working memory has a limited capacity – and the challenges this can present to our children. But are we applying the same knowledge to ourselves? The same negative consequences – impaired cognitive function, increased stress, reduced decision making ability – apply just as much to teachers. The 'Zeigarnik effect' – named after Soviet psychologist Bluma Zeigarnik – identified the predominance our brains place on unfinished tasks (Zeigarnik, 1938). By finding ways to externalise some of this, we can improve our performance and reduce our stress. I've found making a 'done' list is a great way of helping with this. It builds a sense of achievement and focuses you on your successes; far more motivating than the ever growing 'to do' list.

♥ Well moment ♥

At the end of the day or the end of the week, note down everything you have done. Take a moment to congratulate yourself on how incredible that is (and try not to think, 'yes, but I haven't XYZ').

So, what can you make routine? If you are consciously considering every decision, every day, you will not last. Could you have the same lunch every day? Wear the same clothes? Follow the same timings? Anything you can remove from the mental load will help.

Making lists and having systems in place is a great way to remove the need for constant micro decisions. As teachers, this is something we tend to be good at – or get good at pretty quickly. Organisation was a huge theme for the teachers I spoke to. Like Tiffany: 'At the beginning of every half term, I think, what have I got to mark? I do a long-term sort of plan. I plan when I'm going to take work in, when I'm going to mark it, when I'm going to plan lessons for each week, when I'm photocopying – so I don't then have to work at the weekend.' Or Joe: 'I write everything on sticky notes and put them in order. It's really simple, but it helps. If I've got a really busy week, I plan out everything I need to do for each day in my diary and stick by that.'

Planning ahead for these people was crucial – whether it was a week or a term. As Devon said: 'I've learned to be super strategic with my time. Every slot counts. If I don't write it down, it doesn't happen.'

Let's consider the use of technology as well. As Nuren told me: 'If you do something more than three times, a robot can do it. Any repeated task shouldn't really be done by a human.' We may have a way to go with fully integrating technology into education but there are real opportunities with AI to take on the burden of repetitive tasks. How can registration be better automated? What about planning, or feedback?

♥ Well moment ♥

Small wins: five ways to take back control of your time

- Pick your 'non-negotiables' for the week and protect them: going to the gym on Monday or being home for family time on Wednesday; having lunch with a colleague one day or spending 20 minutes outside at lunchtime just chatting with the children.
- Make peace with 'good enough' marking.
- Use a weekly template to timetable repeating tasks.
- Plan when you're not working.
- Say no to something once a week.

Making the load meaningful

Why do you teach? What matters to you? Is it your subject that you are passionate about? Is it the creativity? Is it making a difference for the children – Socially? Emotionally? Academically? Is it the relationships you will build? Is it what you can offer outside the classroom – clubs, sports teams, Duke of Edinburgh?

Identifying this is a great starting point for making the load meaningful. If you spend your time on tasks that you see little value in, it will be soul destroying. If you make sure there is a good sprinkling of tasks you find hugely purposeful and energising, you will feel much better for it. It is not the work per se but the *type* of work you are doing.

As Jodie told me: 'Every week, I try to make sure there's something in my timetable that lights me up – even if it's just one lesson or one club. It keeps me going.' And Devon: 'It's not the work that's draining. It's when you can't see the point of it. I've learned to chase the things that feel like they matter.'

And as the Harvard Study we looked at in Chapter 3 found, meaningful work connects us to our sense of purpose and belonging. It helps us feel competent and valued. All of which is core to long-term wellbeing (Lysova *et al*, 2019).

Conversely, minimising the tasks that offer little value is also important. I appreciate that some of this will be out of your control, but even if you *have* to do it, you can still make decisions about how well it is done. As the saying goes, 'perfection is the enemy of good'. A lot of teachers struggle with this, but why? So often, we were the 'good' students at school. The ones who sat up straight, got the sticker, always did their homework. Lots of teachers have told me, 'I'm a bit of a perfectionist!' Well, I hate to burst your bubble, but perfectionism and teaching do not go hand in hand. Once you accept this, you take back control of where you put your focus and energy. If you don't, you will be pulled from pillar to post. You may be able to convince yourself you are doing it all perfectly, but this won't be the case. You'll just be blind to where you are doing an average job.

The good news is, you don't need to be perfect. It's OK. Being really good at what truly matters will have a far greater impact than trying – and failing – to be perfect at everything. For some things, 'good enough' is… good enough. How do you make those choices? Values are a good place to start, and a great shortcut when making decisions about where to put your limited time and energy. You will have to decide where the balance is between your values and the values of your school. (Hopefully they're fairly well-aligned with yours. If not, you may want to think about whether it is the right school for you.) Research is also a great guide. The research base for what makes the greatest impact on children's learning has grown immeasurably in the last decade. The work of the Education Endowment Foundation (EEF), John Hattie (2009) and so many more has transformed our understanding of the best bets when it comes to directing our time and attention. According to the EEF's 'Teaching and Learning toolkit', you are much better off putting time and energy into metacognitive and self-regulation strategies than you are on parental engagement (2025). So, if you have the time (and the agency), you are better off planning how you build metacognitive strategies into your next lesson than planning a parent workshop. Other high impact strategies include feedback, peer tutoring and collaborative learning. Again, if you can prioritise providing high quality feedback to your students, giving them opportunities to teach each other and creating the conditions for effective group work, all of this can significantly boost learning.

In John Hattie's (2009) meta-analysis of research, one of the greatest effects on children's progress was 'teacher estimates of achievement.' This takes us back to Chapter 2 and the quote attributed to Henry Ford – 'Whether you think you can or whether you think you can't, you're probably right.' According to Hattie (2009), believing that your children can achieve has a far greater impact on their progress than interventions, marking, phonics programmes, or teacher subject knowledge. This is a relatively easy win. You simply have to *believe* that your children can achieve. You have to find that positive inner voice we discussed in Chapter 2 and apply it to them.

I know. I am hugely simplifying the incredible complexity of teaching, schools and education here. Of course, a one-off adjunct on metacognition in a lesson is not going to have a significant impact. But I hope you see the point. Continually considering what will make the greatest difference is an excellent way to separate the wheat from the chaff and spend more time on what really matters. As with so much of what I set out in this book, it is a win-win: the children learn more effectively and your wellbeing improves.

The more you can intentionally consider where to put your time and energy – using research, experience, reflection and colleagues to inform this – the greater the impact you will have (see the 'Teaching Triangle' below for a good starting point with this). The greater the impact, the more meaningful the work is. That is what we are all turning up for every day.

The fact is, you won't remember the emails you answered or the worksheets you printed. You won't remember the lessons you planned or the displays you put up. What you'll remember are those moments of magic (more on those in Chapter 7). The times when you made a real difference. When a child opened up to you. When the learning just came alight. When you found clarity amongst the chaos and you were in your flow state. That's not about ruthless efficiency, it's about making the greatest difference you can. That is enough.

Well practice

The Teaching Triangle:

Draw a triangle and split it into three parts horizontally.

In your top tier you are going to put what matters most. E.g.:

- relationships with children
- high quality modelling
- supporting vulnerable children
- clarity of learning.

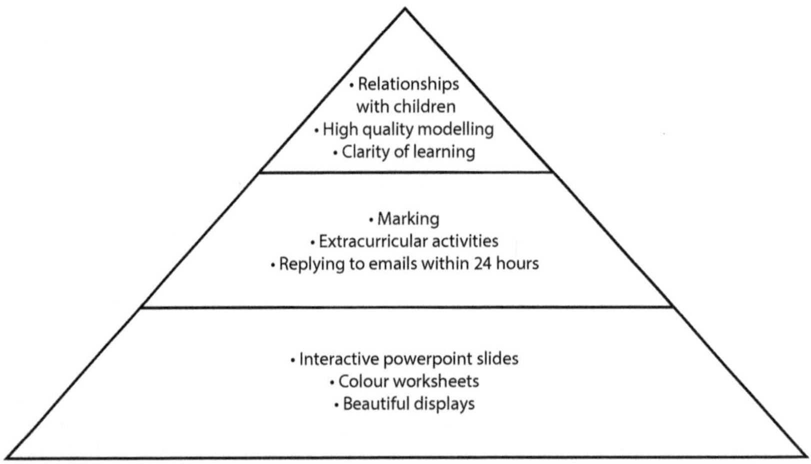

Figure 1 The Teaching Triangle

Key question: What will make the greatest impact on learning or wellbeing today?

In your middle tier you are going to put what is important but can be more flexible. E.g.:

- marking
- extracurricular activities
- replying to emails within 24 hours.

Key question: Does this need doing now and how much focus does it require?

In the bottom tier you are going to put the 'nice-to-haves'. E.g.:

- all singing, all dancing interactive slides
- colour worksheets
- beautiful displays.

Key question: What can I not do or simplify?

Print it and put it somewhere you can see it. When you are feeling overwhelmed or unsure on what to do next, come back to it and use it to help guide your decision making. It may vary during the year, so revisit it regularly for different classes or as your personal situation changes.

Stories from the classroom

Learning to let go

Emma was a lawyer before she became a teacher, and she brought with her the high-stakes pressure of that world. But it didn't take long before she realised teaching required a different mindset. 'You have to learn when to say, "That's enough",' Emma told me. She still works hard, but she's stopped chasing perfection. 'I could keep tweaking a lesson forever, but at some point, I have to ask, "Is it good enough?"' For Emma, clarity came from a shift in values – not everything has to be polished. 'It's not about everything being perfect, it's about being sustainable,' she said.

Emma, secondary school teacher

From overload to order

Kristy remembers the feeling vividly. 'I used to feel totally overwhelmed – like everything was my job.' Early in her career, she tried to do it all, saying yes to every extra task and working long into the evenings. 'I didn't know what to prioritise, and it all felt urgent,' she said. But over time, and with the help of more experienced colleagues, she learned to step back. 'Now I ask myself: what *actually* needs doing right now? What will really make a difference for the kids?' That shift – from reactive to intentional – changed everything. 'I still work hard,' she said, 'but it's on the right things. And I no longer feel guilty about what I haven't done.'

Kristy, primary school teacher

Pacing for the long run

Peter has been teaching for over two decades in the same school. He's seen the highs, the lows and the changes. But what's kept him steady is his approach to the job. 'You've got to find a rhythm that works for you,' he said. Early in his career, he tried to do it all. But experience taught him that sustainability mattered more than perfection. 'It's very easy to get swept up in the urgency of everything, but most of it can wait.' Peter has never pursued senior leadership roles. Instead, he's stayed close to the classroom, mentoring others and working across schools to support teaching practice. 'I still love it,' he said simply. His workload isn't light, but it's manageable – because it's deliberate. 'You learn to tune out the noise and focus on the things that really make the job worthwhile.'

Peter, secondary school teacher

Well reflections

- What can you let burn?
- What do you value most in your classroom?
- How are you intentionally deciding where you put your time and energy today/this week/this term?

Facing the challenges

5 Holding on to yourself

'When we satisfy our needs, we are allowed to fulfil our potential'

(Magness, 2022, p.237).

There is no doubt that, 'putting the children first', sounds great: it's a great moral purpose and perfectly sound. What we really need to ask ourselves is: how do we best do this?

I was recently emailed by Kate who had been tasked with researching workload reduction and had come across our marking policy at Kensington Primary School on the Workload Reduction Toolkit. Her email came through at 9.15 pm. On Sunday night.

'It's for the children', can very easily be a rallying cry for martyrs. In my first school it was given that you bought your own resources, your own laminating pouches, even your own laminator. I've heard countless conversations in which lack of sleep is worn as a badge of honour and becomes a competition, whether it be from late nights planning, marking or resourcing. Of course, I'm not suggesting that we don't make sacrifices for the children: we all do and we all should. The problem starts when those sacrifices become counter-productive. When the belief that marking until the small hours has a greater impact than turning up energised the next day. When another great teacher loses themselves and is driven out of the profession. As Brené Brown sets out in *Daring Greatly* the 'never enough' narrative is one we must all battle against (2015, pp.24–25).

Putting on your oxygen mask

I want you to take a moment and think of a time when you were feeling tired or stressed; judged or lacking in confidence. How were you performing? I'd imagine it's safe to say, not at your best.

Now think about a different day. One when you *were* at your best. Firing on all cylinders. Bulletproof. Unstoppable. Got it? I'd like you to think about how you were feeling then? Can you pinpoint other contextual factors that may have contributed to this different feeling? Was homelife good? Had you recently been on holiday? Did you really like your line manager?

We know that the research says teacher effectiveness is far and away the single biggest factor in children's learning (Hattie, 2009). We focus countless hours and thousands of pounds on monitoring and on CPD to try to improve teaching and learning. But how much do we spend on helping people *be their best*? Just now, when you recalled being at your best, I wager that was as much – if not more – to do with *how* you felt that day as your knowledge or skills.

I'd wanted to call this chapter: 'Being selfish is the most selfless thing you can do'. In the user testing process it seemed to push some buttons. I still feel there is some real wisdom in that provocation however.

If you do not take care of yourself you cannot take care of anyone else

Every year I talk to Year 6 about the vicious SATs cycle. It looks like this:

- I really want to do well in my SATs.
- I worry about doing well in my SATs.
- In worrying about doing well in my SATs, I reduce my ability to do well.
- As a result, I don't do as well in my SATs.
- I end up worrying more.
- I continue to not do as well…

> '…*chronic stress negatively affects the physical and mental health of students and hinders academic performance*'
>
> (Alqurashi, 2023).

There are real parallels here:

- I want to do the best for the children, so I work really hard.
- Working hard means that I'm tired.
- When I'm tired, I don't do as good a job.
- As a result, I work harder.
- Then, I get more tired and now I'm stressed.
- Now I'm not doing as good a job for the children.

And so it continues. Not least because both are driven by the best of intentions.

For teachers, this cycle is pernicious in the short term: turning up exhausted and not able to bring the energy and enthusiasm to lessons, planning, relationships etc. And in the long term, you end up feeling as though you just can't do it anymore. As Joe, a primary school teacher, told me: 'I used to think the best teachers gave everything. Now I think the best ones know when to stop.'

Finding what works for you

When I started at Kensington Primary School, I did not prioritise my own health and wellbeing. At school I'd played lots of sport and been very active, but that fell away at university and never really re-started. By the time I got to Kensington Primary School I was struggling with sleep, inactive, overweight, drinking too much and eating a poor diet. Having moved out of London, walking was no longer part of my daily commute and in my new role I was more desk-based than standing in front of a class. As I mentioned previously, the school was judged by Ofsted as 'requiring improvement.' This Ofsted judgement had happened between me accepting the job and actually starting. Prior to this, the school had been judged as 'good'. On my seventh day we had our Her Majesty's Inspectors (HMI) monitoring visit. I quickly realised that to be successful, first and foremost I would need to work on myself. Leadership also exposed my anxiety and self-doubt: something that had always been in the background but I'd never addressed.

So began a long journey that continues to this day. My physical health has been crucial. First I started cycling. At times I've run. Other times, I've lifted weights. I love to walk. In the ten or so years since I started, I have been consistent in exercising, although the specific type of exercise has varied greatly.

Of equal importance has been my mental and emotional journey. I've done a lot of self-discovery. Mainly through reading and lots of reflective conversations. I've realised a great deal about who I am: my 'introversion'; my anxiety; my competitiveness; my sense of justice (and injustice). I've accepted a lot about myself and made peace with it.

I often describe education as my favourite hobby. There's nothing that interests me more than my work. But the passion so many of us feel is what can become all-consuming if you're not careful. I did feel like I was losing myself at times, particularly with two young children at home. My incredible wife, family and friends all helped. But making sure there was time for me outside of work was also crucial.

Knowing we need time outside of school is one thing. Protecting it is another. What does boundary-setting actually look like in practice?

Boundary setting

For some people it's about emails. I completely understand why this has often become the lightning rod for protecting personal time. Personally, I think it's more about flexibility and compassion. Sometimes I like to wake up and check my emails – although I have intentionally stopped doing this over the past year to support my wellbeing. Having hard and fast email rules can be damaging for people who want to work flexibly around families. It can also have unintentional consequences: a slew of emails arriving at 8.00 am on 'scheduled send' when the official floodgates open. My email signature includes: 'I may choose to send emails early in the morning, late at night, at weekends, or in the school holidays to support my own workload and preferred working patterns. There is no expectation that these are read or responded to outside of normal working hours.'

For some people, it's physically leaving the building early once a week. It might mean saying no to a club or a late meeting, not because you don't care, but because you do. These aren't excuses, they're sustainable, human responses. Boundaries aren't a lack of care. They're an expression of it.

Well practice

Work on setting some professional boundaries. Here are some examples of what they can sound like:

- **'I'd love to help, but I've already committed that time to family.'**
- **'I'm not available then, but I could support during X instead.'**
- **'I've blocked out that evening for rest so I can be ready to go the next day.'**

Of course, it's worth a quick health warning here: balance in all things. Whilst prioritising yourself is key, you remain part of a team. And teaching is not a straightforward 9 to 5. Flexibility, from both sides, allows for a supportive, sustainable work culture. We discussed the importance of vulnerability for better relationships in Chapter 3. Having these conversations, up front and openly with your team, is a great way to show your vulnerability and, as a result, build better relationships.

Well moment

What one boundary do you want to communicate to your team?

- I am going to be more able to talk about anything stressful after my first coffee.
- On a Wednesday it's really important I'm gone by 4.00 pm as that's my time with my daughter.
- I've got a bit of a quirky sense of humour. It really helps me deal with stressful situations. If I ever overstep the mark, please do just tell me.

Making time to be active was always part of it for me. As was time for watching sport, reading, gardening and baking. Time with friends. Time alone. I liked to work hard during the week but switch off over holidays and weekends. Although, as my daughters grow up, that's starting to shift again and a bit of holiday or weekend work is no longer such an issue for me. What is right for you will be unique – as it is for the people I spoke to: one person's kryptonite is another's superpower. It will also change as your life progresses. But whatever stage you are at and whatever it looks like for you, making the time for this is critical.

Well practice: define your edges

To hold onto yourself you need to be clear on where the job ends and you begin. Reflect on:

- What parts of you are non-negotiable? This could be certain times, e.g. evenings; certain characteristics, e.g. values; or certain behaviours, e.g. tone of voice or humour.
- When do you feel most like yourself in school?
- Where do you find your boundaries tested at work?

Use your answers to write your 'edges statement': your red lines that form the basis for separating yourself and your work.

For example: 'After 6.00 pm my attention is for my own family. I always speak to children with compassion and approach issues with curiosity. When I sense guilt, I allow myself to hold that feeling and not jump in with a solution.'

Logically disassembling the guilt

I still wake up at 2.00 am with my mind whirring. That's a work in progress, but I have become considerably more resilient. I am far more able to deal with the stresses and strains in a calm and considered way because I am more balanced.

One of the biggest barriers to achieving this was not the motivation but the guilt. The guilt of putting myself first was almost too much to bear at times. As Jennifer, one of the teachers I spoke to, said: 'There's this weird guilt that creeps in whenever I put myself first.' But when you step back from it, it's illogical.

When I am at my best, I'm amazing. I'm compassionate, sharp-witted, focused, engaging. I say the right thing and do the right thing at the right time. But I was at my best for so little of the time. So I tried to understand why. I invested in my physical health and then my mental health. At the start I hid this. Leaving 'early' was because of a meeting. Taking 10 minutes to meditate was done in the toilet. But the more I invested in myself, the more I saw how much of a difference it made to me. The more I realised this, the more I realised that I needed to share it.

Of course, time is an essential part of this, but so is the emotional investment we all make. Having the depth of relationship, the deep care and love for the children we work with, but maintaining that boundary is exceptionally challenging. Particularly if you are working with children in difficult situations. Many times I've heard teachers say: 'I just want to take them home with me.' Again, being selfish here is crucial. You can make a real, demonstrable difference in children's lives. But you are not their parent/carer. There has to be a line that you do not cross, and you have to hold onto yourself in that. It does not mean you won't cry or that there won't be times your heart hurts for that child, but maintaining perspective is the only way to make it endure.

♥ Well moment ♥

How would you feel if that child – the one you have a special bond with – never came back to school? If the answer is 'broken' or 'devastated' as opposed to 'upset' or 'concerned', maybe you're letting too much of yourself go?

Creating a short mantra can help. Try: 'For the short time they are with me, I am one important part of these children's lives.'

Self-care as professionalism

How to maintain perspective is a lot harder. Self-awareness is a great start. Hayley, a secondary school teacher, told me: 'You can care deeply without giving yourself away.' There's real self-knowledge in that simple statement. Knowing how much of yourself you can give before you become too involved. Sense-checking with colleagues is a great way of doing this. What are they seeing? What would they do in that situation? It's important to check in with yourself as well. None of this is easy, but it is an important part of making the role sustainable and manageable. Teaching is so much more than just a job, but if we don't create boundaries, we will not last in it.

I also think there is a point to make about generational differences and change. Making sweeping comparisons across different times is fraught with difficulty. I am not a social scientist. Lots has been written about Gen Z (those born between 1997 and 2012) and their attitude to work in particular. What I would say is that the world continually changes and teaching as a job has changed immeasurably. What I don't think helps anyone is a culture of blame and recrimination.

At times, listening to people talk, I have been reminded of the classic *Monty Python* sketch, 'The Four Yorkshiremen' (1967). For those of you not familiar with the sketch, it starts with the four aforementioned Yorkshiremen, reminiscing on their humble beginnings. Dressed in tuxedos and drinking fine wine, they begin to compare the poverty of their respective backgrounds. Each time, the comparisons become increasingly ludicrous, trying to outdo one another on their past hardships. Eventually, it's Michael Palin who delivers the final line: 'But you try and tell the young people of today that... and they won't believe ya'.'

I hope you get the point. It's a challenging job. We need to hold each other up and make sure we are all capable of giving our best whilst holding onto ourselves. Blaming the attitudes of the 'younger generation' and comparing it to 'what I used to do' does nobody any favours. Because in the conversations I had with younger teachers, I noticed something that felt quietly radical: a willingness to challenge the inherited norms of the profession. Several spoke about wanting to do the job well without becoming consumed by it. Not out of entitlement, but out of intention. A belief that you can be committed and still have a life outside school. That sustainability matters. As Daniella, a primary school teacher, put it: 'Teaching is a passion of my life, but it can't be my whole life.'

Self-care isn't selfish. It's ultimate professionalism: investment in being the best version of yourself.

Well practice

Let's return to the 'Joy Menu' mentioned in Chapter 2. I want you to compile a list of things that restore, energise or inspire you. Then block out times in the week when you can choose from your menu. This time then needs to be fiercely protected. Here's mine as an example:

Stillness and mindfulness:

- listen to a podcast
- mindful tea or coffee – no phone
- 10 minutes of quiet breathing
- solo walk without a destination.

Connection:

- play a game with Eva and Noa
- share a 'funniest moment of the week'
- cook or eat something with Chloe.

Movement and outdoors:

- go for a run
- walk the dog somewhere new
- sit outside with a drink, book or music.

Creativity and learning:

- read for pleasure
- learn something random
- cook/bake something creative.

Stories from the classroom

Reclaiming her whole self

Early in her career, Daniella felt she had to 'live like a teacher' 24/7 – no parties, no drinks, no weekends off. 'I can't go out. I can't go raving. I'm a teacher,' she told herself. But over time, she realised that the more she denied her personal identity, the less effective she became in the classroom. 'Teaching is a passion of my life,' she said, 'but it can't be my whole life.' Now, she deliberately protects her basic needs – sleep, health, joy – because modelling balance is part of the job. 'If we're teaching kids to take care of themselves, we've got to be doing it too.' It took time, but learning to be herself again helped Daniella rediscover the joy of teaching, too.

Daniella, primary school teacher

From guiding to giving back

Francesca knew she wanted to be a teacher from the age of 15. Even while working in public sector admin, her weekends were filled volunteering with Girlguiding – an outlet for her love of working with young people. Eventually, she took the leap and began her teacher training. She hasn't looked back since. 'I haven't had a day where I've woken up and thought, "I really can't be bothered,"' she said. 'Whatever the class, whatever the lesson, I always look forward to it.' For Francesca, it's all about the connection with her students. 'The joy you see in their eyes when you make that connection... when they finally grasp it, that makes it all worthwhile.' Her path to the classroom wasn't straightforward, but it's where she was always meant to be.

Francesca, secondary school teacher

No more guilt for leaving on time

Lucy used to feel guilty every time she packed up before 5.00 pm – as if being a good teacher meant being the last one in the building. But after reaching the brink of burnout, she shifted. 'You're no good to anyone if you're burned out,' she said. Now, she protects her evenings. She still does a great job, but she also eats dinner with her family. 'I stopped apologising for leaving on time,' she explained. That one act of self-respect transformed her relationship with the role. 'I'm still a good teacher, just one who sleeps and smiles more.'

Lucy, secondary school teacher

Doing less, being better

Sonya used to say yes to everything – extra clubs, mentoring, curriculum work – until her calendar broke her spirit. 'I was doing everything and nothing well,' she said. Eventually, she drew a line. She dropped committees, focused on classroom practice, and started spending more time with her family. The surprise? 'I actually got better at the job.' Saying no didn't diminish her. In fact, it sharpened her. She found joy again. 'I stopped doing everything and focused on doing a few things well,' she reflected. 'That changed everything.'

Sonya, primary school teacher

Well reflections

- What are the basic things I need each week to feel like *me*?
- What am I doing out of guilt or habit?
- Would I encourage my partner/best friend to follow my working habits?

Facing the challenges

6 Keep growing

'If you can't fly then run. If you can't run, then walk. If you can't walk, then crawl, but whatever you do, you have to keep moving'

(Martin Luther King Jr, 1960).

If we want to make teaching work for us, we need to keep moving forward. Stagnation is the enemy of wellbeing. This isn't the same as continually climbing the ladder or moving schools every few years. To grow in teaching, you don't need to do that. It's another reason teaching has the potential to be so beneficial to wellbeing – there are always opportunities to grow and to learn.

The importance of mindset

Paul Dix's (2017) seminal book *When The Adults Change, Everything Changes*, reminds us of the importance mindset plays. Dix's book essentially argues that it is the change in mindset, behaviour and attitude that most positively impacts student behaviour, not rules and systems. Equally, John Hattie's (2009) meta research has consistently shown teacher's belief in their ability to impact student outcomes as the most influential factor in pupil progress (as discussed in Chapter 4). Ultimately: 'Whether you think you can or whether you think you can't, you're probably right' (attributed to Henry Ford).

There's a great video Michael Jordan did for Nike in which he talks about his repeated failures. Arguably the greatest sportsperson of all time talking about how he has missed and lost and failed. But, of course, there's a twist: 'I've missed more than 9,000 shots in my career... I've failed over and over and over again in my life. And that is why I succeed' (Jordan, 2008).

Mindset! Not 'I've let everyone down; I can't do this; I'm no good.' No! Failure is an opportunity for growth. Challenges are opportunities to improve.

As Daniella, a primary school teacher, told me: 'Every morning, I tell myself I'm amazing. And if I think I'm amazing, then I'm amazing. Once you have that confidence and self-assurance that you are the best version of yourself – or you're becoming the best version – it's so much easier to stop the negative coming in, because you know yourself.'

The mindset we hold sets the stage for everything we do. It impacts on our own beliefs and approaches. It directly affects our wellbeing. It supercharges or halts our opportunities for growth. To paraphrase Dix (2017), when our mindset changes, everything changes.

Primed for success

I'm sure this resonates with many of you in relation to the work of Carol Dweck. Her work on 'growth mindset' draws heavily on this thinking, and she posited that our belief in our ability to learn and grow directly influences our actual ability. If we think we cannot achieve something then this will impact the chances of us achieving it (Dweck, 2006).

John Bargh's (1996) work on priming is relevant here. In the study, participants were shown words relating to old age versus a control group. The results demonstrated that those shown the words relating to being elderly walked more slowly after the experiment (Bargh *et al*, 1996). Bargh's work is highly disputed and has ended up as a conductor for the criticism of the social sciences and the challenges of replicating results. Priming as a significant factor in outcomes remains influential.

The 'Pygmalion effect' (Rosenthal & Jacobson, 1968) describes the idea that high expectations lead to improved outcomes. It is what 'adaptive practice' is built upon. By putting children on the 'high achieving' table or in the top set, we are priming them: telling them that we have high expectations and that they are capable in a specific subject (or subjects). As teachers, we will also – often unconsciously – treat them differently. We will use subtly different language, our body language will change, we'll interact with them differently. All of this will help to cement their beliefs about their agency and their ability to improve. In turn, this will directly impact upon their progress.

In education the 'Pygmalion effect' is often also referred to as the 'Rosenthal effect'. In 1968, Rosenthal and Jacobson administered a 'new test' to a group of elementary school students. This test was cutting edge and could accurately predict which children had the capacity to make rapid academic progress. The only thing was, it was a complete fabrication. The children were all randomly assigned as either 'intellectual bloomers' or not, based on 'the outcomes of the test'. All the teachers were told which children had the capacity to learn at a faster rate. At the end of the year, those children who had been identified as having the capacity to learn more effectively had made significantly more progress than their peers (Rosenthal & Jacobson, 1968).

As Fozia, a secondary school teacher, said: 'Especially when kids aren't very confident, it's so nice to see them come out of their shell – they just need somebody to believe in them. [...] As a teacher, you need to look at the bigger picture. I think relationships are 100 per cent the key – you have to get the kids on side. [...] Treat them like younger adults and take an active interest in them... Once you've developed that relationship, they don't just see you as their maths teacher. They see you as a member of staff who is here to help them.'

A counterpart to the 'Pygmalion effect' was identified in Rosenthal's later work with Jacinto Inbar and Elisha Baband. The 'Golem effect' (1983) demonstrated that negative expectations have a negative impact on progress. Again, this is part of a self-fulfilling prophecy – where those who see themselves as less capable live down to those expectations – as a result of interactions, decisions and approaches differing consciously or unconsciously. For example, asking questions that require less thought or treating behavioural cues differently (Baband *et al*, 1982).

Ultimately, by cultivating a mindset that supports growth, we can significantly affect the potential for us to grow and develop in our roles.

♥ Well moment ♥

Priming

Choose three words that you will use to prime your mindset and put them where you can see them throughout the day, e.g. courageous; compassionate; ambitious. You could even get your class involved. Write up these words and display them up above the classroom door.

It's not fair!

The other crucial part here is your agency in all of this. I always saw myself as self-motivated, driven, a problem solver. And I am. But I can also fall into the trap of being a victim. Learning to shift my mindset has had a really positive impact.

Health warning: What I am about to set out can be deeply challenging. When I was initially faced with taking on the role of victim in certain situations, I found it really difficult. I want to be really clear here. None of this is about blame. Nor is it saying there is never injustice. And it certainly isn't saying it's your fault!

However, these shifts in mindset are a key tool in helping you thrive and grow as a teacher over the course of your career. If you can develop a real sense of agency and can see challenges as opportunities for growth. If you can frame situations positively and prime your thinking for success. If you can reflect on what you achieved, not what you didn't; what you did well, not what went wrong, then you will transform your wellbeing and make a challenging job a sustainable and more enjoyable one.

The *Drama Triangle* was first described by psychiatrist Stephen Karpman in the 1960s. In it, he set out three roles we could play: victim, rescuer or persecutor. In the victim role we feel powerless. Life is happening to us. We have no or very little agency to do anything about it. This is because of a persecutor. The persecutor could be a person or a situation. As the victim, we look for a rescuer to help us solve the problem (Karpman, 1968).

'It's Friday afternoon and I (the victim) have been asked to hand in some data analysis on Monday by my line manager (the persecutor). I was planning a restful weekend and really needed to recharge after a tough week – and they knew this! My partner teacher (the rescuer) understands. They agree it is completely unreasonable and my line manager shouldn't be allowed to do this and should be more considerate.'

Even writing the above example, I can feel my sense of injustice bubbling up. It is unfair! They are unreasonable! When someone first challenged me on presenting as a victim, I was furious. 'How dare they! I work so hard! I'm not a victim.' Sure, people are unreasonable at times and situations are unfair, but that's not my fault.

The point isn't about right or wrong. It's not whether the Phase Leader in this example is or isn't unreasonable. It's about you: the choices you have in this situation and the agency to decide what you do next. If you follow my train of thought above (the victim's thought process) you likely end up feeling helpless and frustrated. The rescuer then reinforces this feeling – 'you're right, this is unfair'. Only by following a different thought process and considering the situation differently can you regain agency and work towards a positive solution. In this example, it may just need a quick conversation and perhaps the Phase Leader would realise it was not a reasonable request and agree a different deadline. Or, you may need to be more assertive about boundaries, timeliness of requests and reasonable expectations. There are multiple possible ways forward but all of them require you to take on a different role to that of victim.

> *'Schools are a place of learning for everybody, and you just need to take opportunities. Opportunities present themselves everywhere, all the time, and it's just your job to take them by the hand, you know, and grasp them and do them. And I think that's something that keeps me going as well. I'll always look for the opportunities.'*
>
> (Jennifer, secondary school teacher)

Let's be clear here. None of this is about being a doormat or overly passive. It certainly doesn't mean you should lie down in the face of injustice: reframe it, smile and dust yourself off! Nor does it mean that you should ignore the issues, pull your socks up, stiffen that upper lip, and keep calm and carry on. No! That's the whole point, it's not about 'them', it's about you. Is getting upset helping you? Do you feel better being frustrated? Are you achieving more by thinking that you can't because the world is against you? By taking back control, realistically identifying where you do have power, looking for solutions, and priming your thinking to be optimistic and positive, you will greatly improve your own situation.

In the 'empowerment dynamic,' developed by David Emerald as the counterpoint to Karpman's Drama Triangle, Emerald encourages us to move from:

- Victim to Creator
- Persecutor to Challenger
- Rescuer to Coach

As Creator you are taking control of your situation. You are focused on what you want to achieve, not blaming others or dwelling on problems. In this mindset, people or events don't make you feel a certain way, you have *choice* over how you respond. The priorities are the outcomes you want to achieve, not the barriers you face. And challenges are opportunities, not threats (Emerald, 2005).

Harnessing this way of thinking can significantly improve your day-to-day life and make a significant difference professionally and personally. It can also be the key to your growth.

Well practice: be the Creator, not the Victim

Reflect back on your week. Was there a time when you were in 'victim mode'? What happened? How did you feel? What was the outcome? Note down your answers.

This coming week, try to catch yourself when you start to think like a Victim. Pause. Intentionally choose to be the Creator instead. What happens? How do you feel? What is the outcome? Note down your answers.

Repeat this exercise a few times. Reflect on your answers. Are there any patterns? How do the two approaches impact on the outcome you would like? How do the two approaches affect your wellbeing?

Why growth matters

Habits are hugely powerful. James Clear's book, *Atomic Habits,* is a bestseller for good reason. We explored the importance of habits in making teaching manageable in Chapter 4. And yet, there is a risk associated with habits. It is easy to become reliant on our habits, but those habits can create entropy and stagnation (Clear, 2018). Before we know it, we're the person resisting new ways of thinking and working. We're the ones saying, 'but this is how I've always done it', and in the process we've professionally stalled.

Finding ways to continue growing professionally is hugely important to your ongoing wellbeing. In teaching – and in work in general – growth is often equated with promotion. This is challenging, for all professions. So many people lose connection with what they love and why they chose the profession in order to climb the ladder and, ultimately, manage people. A good friend of mine was a brilliant designer. Deeply passionate about his work, he was very successful. He started his own company. It grew. Before he knew it, his job was HR, finance, sales, marketing and leadership. He was proud of what he had achieved, but he'd lost connection with what he loved and what energised him.

I've heard this story so many times. From teachers, but also from people across all industries. It's really tough because we reward this type of growth financially. So I certainly don't want to make assumptions or preach from my ivory tower. We all make our choices. But there are other choices. It doesn't have to be teacher > middle leader > SLT > headteacher. What is crucial is that a) you make a conscious choice based on a deep understanding of what matters to you and b) you keep growing and developing in some way. As previously mentioned, there are so many opportunities for this in teaching. We've vastly expanded our knowledge of cognitive science over the past 10 years. Our understanding of special educational needs and disabilities and how to support children with these in the classroom is almost endless. You can also run an after school or lunchtime club on pretty much anything. Or you can support with fundraising and the PTA. You could also be a staff governor. The fact is, there are endless opportunities to grow and develop.

Learning new skills is one of the *5 ways to mental wellbeing* outlined by the NHS (2022). Once again, teaching provides an opportunity to positively contribute to your overall wellbeing.

♥ Well moment: curiosity ♥

Observe a colleague and take one thing they do that you can replicate and make your own.

Growing from the inside out

We've explored the mindset required to grow. Developing this mindset is in itself a form of personal growth. By developing the way you think and the way you approach situations, you will develop as a practitioner. As we explored in Chapter 5, how you feel is often more important than what you know. So how else can we invest in ourselves and keep growing?

We often consider 'professional development' to be about subject knowledge and pedagogy. You *might* get some 'leadership development' if you are taking on a leadership role. Potentially, that leadership development may include some elements of looking at yourself: how you think; what you believe; what influences your decision making. But that is not the norm and, as a teacher, it is very rare that this will be the focus of your Monday night training.

Yet, personal internal growth is not just hugely significant for your practice, but also for your sense of achievement and fulfilment. Developing a greater sense of self, challenging your beliefs, and becoming increasingly self-aware are all fantastic ways to continue to professionally develop. By doing this, you can become both a better teacher *and* improve your wellbeing. The bonus here is that all of this growth has the potential to impact your personal life just as much as your professional. How, then, can you do this?

Reflective practitioners

Being reflective is drilled into teachers. We're always looking at what could be improved, what we'd do differently next time, which children found a task too easy/challenging/boring. In Chapter 2, we explored negativity bias and the dangers of this. But when focused on our internal monologue, reflection is a powerful, intentional and transformative tool.

However you choose to do so, carving out 10 minutes each week to reflect on the thought processes, emotions and beliefs that most impacted your practice is a great way to start developing a conscious understanding of your inner voice. Some people love to journal, others prefer debriefing with a friend, partner or colleague.

Well practice: intentional reflections

Try using these questions to help frame your thinking:

- When was I most energised this week? Why was that?
- How did I respond to that challenge? Why was that?

- How was it similar/different to how I responded to that challenge last week? Why?
- What story did I tell myself this week that turned out to be inaccurate? Why did I tell myself that story? How did I find out it was inaccurate? What could I have done differently?

The more you can deeply reflect and get to the heart of your thinking – from the position of a Creator not a Victim – the more you can develop your understanding of what underlying factors influence your thinking and the more you can start to develop them, helping you to continue growing as a practitioner and a person.

Breaking the habit

As we discussed, habits are great. However, entrenched, immovable habits can become a hefty ball and chain, weighing us down. Habits of mind are particularly insidious as they are far less tangible. Finding opportunities to shine a light on these internal habits can help us hold onto the ones that help and change or drop the ones that have become barriers to growth.

Well practice: habits of mind

Each half-term, find a habit of mind. These will often be framed as limiting statements:

- I can't speak up in meetings.
- This child can't make progress.
- I can't change how we plan.

Reframe this using your Creator mindset and prime yourself for success. Set yourself achievable goals that are within your area of influence:

- I am going to say one thing in tomorrow's meeting.
- I am going to observe this child, try a new approach and reflect on why it did/didn't work. If it didn't work, I am going to use that to help inform the next approach.
- I am going to come up with a clear rationale for why it would be good to plan differently, gather evidence, and share this with my subject lead.

As you look to make changes, particularly changing habits, remember: change is challenging and if it doesn't work, it's not a failure or a disaster; it's an opportunity for further reflection and further growth.

We've looked at how to keep growing internally. Now we're going to explore how to keep growing externally – the visible skills and knowledge; what we commonly refer to as *Continuing Professional Development* (CPD).

Growing from the outside in

I've deliberately focused on *internal* growth first because I see time and again that there is far less emphasis put on this in the professional development of teachers. Despite internal growth having the potential to be more transformational, the vast majority of our limited time goes into external growth, i.e. the development of our knowledge and skills, predominantly around curriculum and pedagogy with some behaviour and safeguarding thrown in for good measure. Internal growth is really important in priming ourselves for external growth. In turn, external growth is vital in our ongoing growth journey.

Daniel Pink's (2010) seminal work on intrinsic motivation, *Drive*, boils the concept of growth down to three key elements: purpose, autonomy and mastery. This is echoed in Steve Magness' *Do Hard Things*, a book on building resilience (2022). Magness clearly expounds the importance of domain knowledge here: 'When the work is done in the name of getting better, of enjoying the process, of searching for mastery of the craft, then confidence gradually grows' (Magness, 2022, p.81).

The reality is, confidence, the ability to thrive and the sense of 'a job done well' all come from actually having the skills and knowledge to *do* the job well. Our negativity bias, victim mindset and negative priming can all trip us up even when we *are* doing a good job. However, if we just don't have the knowledge and skills necessary to actually do this, no amount of positivity, hope or priming are going to help our wellbeing. Ongoing investment in your skills and knowledge is key.

Professional development in teaching is considered so important that there is a huge amount of time and energy invested in it. Whole organisations such as the Chartered College of Teaching have been founded on the basis of supporting teachers' ongoing professional development. I am not about to try and summarise that here or suggest the best ways to invest in your professional development. However, I would suggest six guiding principles to keep in mind that will help you to grow professionally, which in turn will help you to keep engaged, motivated, enthused and thriving. You don't need to follow them all religiously. Maybe choose one or two and consider how they can help evolve your approach to growth.

Well practice: professional development guiding principles

1. **Depth over breadth:** Attaining mastery in specific areas is both more motivating and has a greater impact than a broad brush, surface knowledge of everything.
2. **Focus on what interests you:** Development that is relevant and relatable to what already intrigues you will be more engaging – what connects with your values or a specific challenge you're facing?
3. **Take charge:** Some of your professional development will be directed by your school but there is so much information available: books, social media, colleagues – direct your own development.
4. **Make it social:** There's a million people employed in education in this country and many more working for organisations that are interested in education. Education – and professional development – are not the sole preserve of schools. Find people who are interesting and interested, and talk to them about whatever it is that is inspiring or fascinating you right now.
5. **Take risks**: Your classroom is a great place to learn. Close-to-practice research – trialling out new ideas and then reflecting on them – is a brilliant way to develop your skills and knowledge. Even better if you can make it social.
6. **Think as well as do:** Rest is critical for learning. Find time and space to allow all of the above to sink in.

Investment in your professional self is an excellent way to improve your wellbeing. As Magness says: 'Self-esteem and confidence go hand in hand. They only work if they're founded in reality' (Magness, 2022, p.70).

The fact is, the best teachers don't have all the answers, they have the mindset to keep on asking better questions.

Keep on growing. It's how we keep the spark alive, bring hope and positivity, and stay connected to the children and ourselves. It will also help improve your wellbeing in all areas of your life.

Stories from the classroom

Mutual learning

Aisha shared how every class teaches her something. 'Every year, I learn more from the children than they probably learn from me,' she laughed. She described how one child challenged her to think differently about behaviour – not as defiance, but as communication. 'He helped me realise I needed to listen more deeply,' she said. Now in her tenth year of teaching, Aisha sees growth not as moving up, but as moving deeper. 'Teaching humbles you,' she said. 'That's where the learning is.'

Aisha, primary school teacher

The art of knowing when to step back

Malcolm reflected on a moment in his career when he was instructed not to answer pupils' questions during a problem-solving lesson. At first, he hated it. 'It went against my instincts,' he said. 'I just wanted to help.' But over time, he learned the power of stepping back. 'Sometimes, growth means resisting the urge to rescue,' he explained. He now coaches others to distinguish between when pupils need guidance – and when they need space to struggle. According to Malcom, that nuanced judgement comes only with time and reflection.

Malcolm, secondary school teacher

Growth as a way of life

Hannah radiates growth mindset. Alongside teaching full-time and leading her department, she's studying for a doctorate and learning Italian. 'I'm always developing, as a teacher and as a person,' she said. But growth isn't just about collecting qualifications. For Hannah, it's embedded in everyday practice: through curriculum design, interdisciplinary planning and structured time for reflection. 'It's about creating space to think,' she explained. 'Every year, I learn new ways to teach better – and be better.' That slow, steady refinement is what has kept her energised.

Hannah, secondary school teacher

Well reflections

- Where in your job do you 'think you can't'? Why?
- Where in your job do you 'think you can'? Why?
- Can you remember a time you 'grew' professionally and it positively impacted on your wellbeing? Why was that?

7 The moments that stay with you

'The problem… is not that we have a short life, but that we waste time'

(Seneca, 2018, p.7).

'...this question of mattering, of leaving something for future generations…it's about what we mean to other people'

(Waldinger & Schulz, 2023, pp.277–278).

- What is a 'life well-lived'?
- What are we here for?
- What are we trying to achieve in our time on this rock?
- And why might teaching be uniquely placed to be a fundamental part of the answer to these questions?

Hopefully, the preceding chapters have given you a combination of practical tips and guidance on how the profession is not just something to endure, but a key aspect to thriving in your life. The final three chapters will explore the concept of a 'good life' more broadly and how teaching can be a key part of this.

The good life

What is life? Ultimately, when we look back, life is simply a collection of the memories we have. So, the quality of your life is dependent on the quality of your memories. It follows then, that a 'good life' is one filled with 'good' memories.

If one part of a 'good life' is about creating good memories, then I would argue that teaching is a wonderful career to direct your working time and energy to. The sense of purpose, the relationships, the joy. All the moments that stay with you.

When I look back at my life after the age of 21, there is much that stands out. Of course, memory is complex and it varies at different times. However, it is fair to say that what I remember from before teaching is predominantly from my personal life. The time since I started teaching is far more balanced with both personal and professional memories.

I remember my first class as an Early Career Teacher (ECT) vividly. The names of the students, their faces, their personalities. I remember doing a topic on Banksy and one of them using a spray can to paint their own face (I then had to apologise to the very understanding parents!) My ECT class was a Year 2 class and I remember our production of *Oliver!*, where one of the children sung a solo. Not a dry eye in the house!

I remember taking our school football team all the way through the Premier League competition and winning. They were even on Sky Sports, and we travelled to the Riverside Stadium in Middlesborough for the final. One of the boys went on to play for Tottenham. A truly magical experience for everyone involved.

One moment I particularly remember, that weaves the personal and professional, was 16 December 2011, a Friday. My eldest daughter, Eva, had been born the day before. My wife and I had decided that I would go into school that day as it was the last day of term (I could then have four wonderful weeks with her and Eva). We all filed into the hall for the end of term assembly and the children got up to sing Coldplay's 'Christmas Lights'. I'm deeply moved by children singing on any day, but on that day I could not fight back the tears. In fact, I'm actually crying as I sit here and write this! Just to finish it off – and this is 100 per cent true – I looked out of the window and the snow had just started to fall. A truly magical memory that will stay with me forever.

Well practice: the power of stories

Stories are a great way to reinforce memories.

- This half-term, keep a look out for one really meaningful moment: a child's breakthrough; a moment of real joy; a positive interaction. Then, tell that story. Tell a friend. Tell your family. Tell a colleague. Tell yourself.

Saying it out loud reinforces the impact and gives it real weight. It stops it from just floating away with all of the other moments.

I remember school fetes, plays, sporting events, dances, and so much more. I even remember the odd Maths or English lesson I taught. So many moments of true joy and difference. And I remember the children, and their families. I remember a particular group of Year 6 children. As so often is the case, they weren't the best behaved or the academically strongest. But they had real character. It was my 40th birthday. Someone put on 'Celebrate' and we were all up dancing. 600 odd children and me. They did some amazing performances as well. Incredible dance routines. Those children hold a special place in my heart.

I know that when I finally hang up my boots, I will look back with genuine pride at what I did and I will have so many memories to sustain me when I am no longer doing it anymore. Surely that is a fundamental part of a 'good (working) life'?

Well moment

- **Memory message:** Write an email to yourself about the positive memories from this term. Schedule it to send a year from now.
- **Total recall:** Take time to consciously recall a moment you made a difference and play it back in your mind.
- **Magic moments:** On paper or on your phone, start noting down those magic moments. Go back to them regularly and tell the stories.

Of course, there are moments we carry with sadness too. Times we wished we had acted differently, words we wish we'd said. Telling my ECT class our headteacher had passed away was incredibly hard. A child I remember from a Year 5 class who was struggling and I just did not know how to best deal with him. But it is these challenges that are the greatest opportunities for growth and development. Facing up to my limitations. Holding onto those moments when I wished I had been a better version of myself. Knowing that I did my best at that time, but wanting to do better if I had the chance again. Those memories have all been a crucial part of my development and my career.

Well practice: dealing with challenge

Teaching is full of challenges. One of these is that you are making hundreds of decisions every day. It's easy to beat ourselves up and obsess about those we feel didn't go well and what we'd do differently next time.

One trick I've used is to imagine how I will feel about a decision or situation in 5 weeks, 5 months and 5 years. The reality is, 5 weeks/months/years ago there

would have been lots of worries you had, which felt just as 'big' and challenging as those you're worrying about now. But you can't even remember what they were! Imagine how you'll feel about this situation in the future and it helps diminish the all-encompassing nature of any fear, anxiety, or dread you may have.

And, of course, there are the moments we create for the children. The smile that made a difference; the moment of kindness; the intellectual breakthrough. Whether it's building confidence; inspiring them to go above and beyond; tapping previously untapped potential; or just being there and being consistent. The impact teachers have on children's lives resonates far beyond the classroom. We'll explore this further in the next chapter.

So why do certain moments stay with us? Research suggests part of this is related to the emotional resonance of events (McGaugh, 2003). Emotionally intense or resonant events activate longer-term storage in the brain. There is further research showing that events which have meaning are more likely to be stored as memories (Conway & Pleydell-Pearce, 2000). As teachers, you will have been deluged with theories and professional development on the construction and decay of memory. It is worth reflecting on this though. Those memories we hold onto are the ones that really mean something to us. If a good life is one constructed of positive memories, then spending our time working in an area that has real emotional resonance is crucial to creating those memories.

Teaching, more than most other professions, gives you moments of joy and laughter as well as profound sadness and heartbreak. All of these can anchor you to your purpose. They are the rich tapestry of our lives and they give us both meaning and direction. The sheer depth and range of those moments are what give our lives real meaning. Sure, a life where you turn up, clock in, clock out *ad infinitum* may be easier, but is that truly what you want from your life? Is that how to make the most of your time on this mortal coil? As Diane Ackerman says, '...the love affair with life, is to live as variously as possible' (1991, p.309).

Well practice: making memories

Plan a lesson, visit, experience or opportunity entirely focused on making magical memories – for you and the children. When it's done, write down all of the positive memories you have of the event. Reflect back on them at least once a week for the next term.

For all those wonderful memories that you have, there are so many more to be made. Ultimately, we remember how people made us *feel*, not what they did. In that sense, maybe a life spent teaching – creating memories for us and for others – is a life very well lived?

Of course, it's not just me. Every teacher I spoke to had their own vivid, unforgettable memories of the moments that resonated with them. Here are just a few.

Stories from the classroom

Putting students first, no matter what

As a secondary headteacher, Malcolm has faced every crisis imaginable, but one incident will stay with him forever. A serious allegation arose that one student had harmed another, triggering a police investigation. Practically overnight, Malcolm had to rearrange the entire school day to ensure the two students never crossed paths, all while providing both academic and emotional support. 'Education wasn't important for a while; their welfare was,' he recalled. The situation was a nightmare: separate schedules, special supervision, endless meetings with distraught families. But Malcolm and his team poured their hearts into helping the victim feel safe and regain her footing. Months later, on results day, that same girl opened her exam envelope with a grin of triumph. Despite everything, she had earned the grades she needed to move forward. Malcolm watched her celebrate and felt tears in his eyes. 'It's those kids who've had struggles that I find most motivating,' he told me. Supporting a young person through trauma and seeing her come out the other side; to Malcolm, that is the pinnacle of why he became a teacher.

Malcolm, secondary school headteacher

A student finds his spark

Adam's proudest success story is a boy who once hated PE but now absolutely loves it. When the student joined in Year 7, he dragged his feet in every sports lesson and never participated willingly. Adam made it his mission to connect with this quiet boy. He discovered the student liked dance and rhythm, so Adam incorporated more music and movement into class and praised the boy's every small win. Over the years, the boy's confidence grew bit by bit. By the time he reached Year 11, he was voluntarily staying after school to play badminton and even helping Adam coach younger students. At the leavers' assembly, this student publicly thanked 'Mr Heath' for not giving up on him. Adam was deeply moved. He had watched a child transform from disengaged to passionate by feeling seen and supported. 'When he gets older, he'll remember PE lessons fondly,' Adam reflected. Knowing that he helped a young person discover enjoyment in being active is a reward no exam result could ever match.

Adam, secondary school PE teacher

'Earth sausage' – a lesson in confidence

Guy has a quirky trick that once helped a student overcome a serious fear. As a veteran secondary school teacher (and deputy head of a boarding house), he mentored a sixth form girl who was preparing for an important presentation – a make-or-break part of her International Baccalaureate. This student was bright but had a speech impediment; she lisped on her 's' sounds and was terrified of speaking in front of others. Seeing her distress, Guy drew inspiration from the movie *The King's Speech*. He coached her one afternoon, sharing a technique: instead of hissing out 's' directly, start with another sound. 'Don't say "sss" – roll into it with a word like "saus-age,"' he advised with a smile. To remind her, Guy scrawled the words **'Earth sausage'** on a huge poster and taped it to the back wall of his classroom. It was nonsense, sure, but it made her laugh and relax. During her presentation, whenever she felt nerves rising, she glanced over the audience's heads at that silly sign and remembered to ease her pronunciation. She absolutely nailed it: she was clear, confident, and charismatic. A few years later, that same young woman ran for public office and asked Guy to help canvas for her campaign, a gesture that nearly brought him to tears. It all started with a little creativity and compassion on Guy's part. Seeing a student transform her self-confidence and succeed was, as he put it, 'wonderful…that's why I love what I do.'

Guy, secondary school teacher and boarding house leader

Unleashing a hidden talent

Hannah thrives on designing interdisciplinary projects, and nothing proves their value more than students like the boy she met last year. This student had severe ADHD; in traditional classes he could hardly sit still for five minutes or focus on instructions. Hannah often had to call his name repeatedly to keep him on task. Then came the term's big interdisciplinary project – a blend of art, technology, and ethics – posing the question, 'Should we embrace AI?' Students could choose how to present their answer. This particular boy decided to build a futuristic classroom model out of craft materials. The transformation was astonishing. He became *laser-focused*. He sketched designs, brought in recyclable materials from home, and even taught himself to 3D print tiny furniture for his model. Hannah and her colleagues watched in awe at this child happily pouring hours of effort into an academic project. At the end-of-term exhibition, he proudly showed off a detailed diorama with robots and students learning side by side. His explanation of his stance on AI was insightful and passionate. Hannah was blown away. She knew he had it in him, but the project-based approach was the key to unlocking that potential. Moments like this, she said, 'are the most rewarding things.' It reinforced her belief that given the right environment, every student can find their spark and shine.

Hannah, Head of Interdisciplinary Projects

Sisterly spats

One morning, Aisha faced two pupils who bickered constantly. She nearly separated them, but realised 'they basically fight like siblings… if they're not going to be a bit silly, then they're not children.' Instead of coming down harshly, Aisha told them, 'Guys, you lot are like sisters. You're literally fighting and kicking, but you still care about each other.' The girls eventually giggled, and their friendship emerged stronger. Aisha's patience turned a classroom conflict into a lesson in understanding. In another instance, a quiet student grew extremely attached to Aisha. On the last day of term, the student teared up and told her, 'I wish, miss, that you would just adopt me and take me home at the end of the year.' It brought Aisha to tears, but in a happy way as she realized the safe haven she provided. 'This child found her happy space. She was able to be herself and loved coming to school,' Aisha recounted. Moments like these, from diffusing 'sisterly' spats to being an emotional anchor for a child in need, reaffirmed Aisha's belief that as a teacher she guides not just academics but the formation of kind, caring young people.

Aisha, primary school teacher

A personal transformation formed from tragedy

Early in her career, Daniella often felt like she was in survival mode, struggling with self-doubt. A few years on, and she's grown into a remarkably confident teacher and a beloved figure to her pupils. One memory in particular fuels her sense of purpose. A little girl in Daniella's class lost her mother very suddenly over the Christmas holidays. The child was distraught, yet as soon as she returned to school, Daniella saw her brighten. She clung to her teacher, telling Daniella softly, 'My mummy's not here anymore, but I'm so happy that you're here with me.' Daniella will never forget the look on the girl's face. The child was sadness at home, but pure comfort at school. It hit Daniella that *she* was that child's rock. 'Whenever she came to school, everything was happy for her,' Daniella recalled. Being that constant in a child's life affirmed why she teaches. Daniella also underwent her own transformation. She realized she needed to believe in herself the way she believes in her students. Now each morning before class, Daniella looks in the mirror and tells herself, 'I'm amazing.' It might sound silly, but it works. 'If I think I'm amazing, then I'm amazing.' This daily ritual of self-affirmation has bolstered her confidence. Instead of focusing on mistakes or negatives, she radiates positivity, and her students feed off it. Daniella's journey from self-doubt to self-love, and from being a teacher to an *anchor* in her students' lives, illustrates the profound emotional impact teachers can have.

Daniella, primary school teacher

Well reflections

- What moment from your teaching life do you still think about?
- When have you been surprised by your own emotional reaction?
- How do you make space to notice and remember those moments that will last a lifetime?

Reimagining the role

8 The ripple effect

'O Captain. My Captain!'

(Whitman, 1865)

In the Department for Education's 'Get Into Teaching' advert, the teacher is portrayed as a life-changing hero. Children cheering, one child clearly going through a lot whose life he turns around; opportunities to be the caped crusader of children's lives (Department of Education, 2023).

Dead Poets Society gives us our greatest cultural anti-establishment teaching hero: Robin Williams, surrounded by his pupils standing on their desks as they recite 'O Captain! My Captain!' by Walt Whitman.

The fact is, we remember the grand gestures. The moments of rebellion. The transformations. They pull at the heart strings. They get the blood pumping faster. They are exciting and they are emotional. But it's easy to get caught up in them, to see 'leaving a legacy' as a giant, one-off transformation.

The small things

In his book, *Legacy,* James Kerr (2013) talks about the New Zealand rugby team, the All Blacks. One of the key elements he highlights are the small actions they take that make the difference. He talks about the team 'sweeping the sheds' after all their adoring supporters have gone home: literally clearing up all of the empty coffee cups and burgers wrappers that have been left behind. It is these everyday actions that build their legacy. This is done through humility, contributing to the team and turning up every day to make a difference (Kerr, 2013).

For me, this resonates deeply with what teaching is really like, away from the movies and TV ads. So often, it is the little things you do that really change lives.

I asked my daughter Eva to cast her mind back. What was it that a teacher had done that really made a difference for her? She talked about Mrs Constant, her Year 6 teacher, who noticed her love of maths and continually pushed her to take on more challenging work. Currently in Year 8, Eva has just qualified for the next round of the national maths awards. Her ultimate goal: to study Maths at Cambridge. Who knows where that might lead? I'm delighted my daughter has found something that she really loves. And I am hugely grateful to Mrs Constant and her other teachers who noticed and supported that spark. (For the record, Eva is much more interested in being a dancer than a mathematician at the moment.)

So much of the difference you make is in those small gestures. Saying good morning to a child. Really seeing them. Taking the time to connect; taking an interest. Noticing they have an aptitude for something, or conversely if they are struggling with something. To some extent, if it was purely about the magic moments, that might be easier. But it's not. You never know if your one decision, your one chat, or your throwaway comment might be the moment that makes the greatest difference for that child. What is the potential ripple effect from that moment?

♥ Well moment ♥

Make a list of three students you've struggled to connect with. What's one thing you could ask them today that isn't about behaviour or work?

A lasting impact

Many celebrities share stories about the difference teachers made to their lives. Former Children's Laureate Cressida Cowell MBE (2019) has praised her teacher Miss Mellows and her instrumental role in shaping Cowell's self-belief: 'Sometimes, that is what you want as a child, someone to recognise your passion. It is really important that you have teachers who tell you there is something you might be quite good at.' From simple gestures, to Children's Laureate.

Musician John Legend (2017) has talked about the impact his English teacher Mrs Bodey had on him. Her simple belief and encouragement in his ability to write started the process that ended with him being one of the world's greatest living artists.

Oprah Winfrey (2023) has often talked about her fourth grade teacher, Ms Duncan, who created a spark for learning in her. This gave her the drive and the belief to achieve everything she has since.

There are so many stories like this. These in particular get coverage because they involve celebrities. But the fact is, so many people have their story of a teacher who made a real difference in their lives. These stories are never about a lesson or some particularly skilled pedagogy. They are not about exam results or revision. They are not about the data or the marking. They are always about belief and about connection. How their teacher really seeing them was what made the difference. Francesca, one of the teachers I spoke to, told me: 'It's when a kid turns around and says, "Thanks, Miss, you're my favourite teacher." Maybe they say it to everyone, but it still fills you with pride. It makes you think "I can do this, it is definitely worthwhile".'

With great power comes great responsibility

Equally, many children do not have this story. Or worse, their story is not of a teacher who made a positive difference but a *negative* one. In some cases, this is what inspired them. Those stories of hardship, a teacher telling them they could or would not, spurred them on. Like Betty Campbell, the first black headteacher in Wales. In an interview with the BBC, Campbell recalled telling her headteacher that she too wanted to teach. His response was, 'Oh my dear, the problems would be insurmountable'. She said: 'I went back to my desk and I cried. That was the first time I ever cried in school. But it made me more determined; I was going to be a teacher by hook or by crook' (Campbell, 2019).

Unlike almost any other profession, you have a chance to impact people's lives as a teacher. Not just children. So much of what happens in those formative years echoes through the rest of our lives. It is a huge responsibility but also an incredible opportunity. By making simple choices, day after day, you can truly change lives for the better. Not many other jobs give you that opportunity. It is worth holding onto and keeping sight of this, because this chance to make a difference is part of what makes for a good life. That all contributes to improved personal wellbeing.

All of this happens without fanfare. No one is standing on a desk and no one is cheering or quoting Whitman. It doesn't happen in a moment. Turning up each day, being a human being, trying to find ways to understand, unlock and build that connection; that is what ripples through the lives of the young people you work with.

Wellbeing step-by-step

Finding and maintaining positive wellbeing is far from easy. It takes incredible skill, resilience, dedication and commitment. Children can be challenging, and the most challenging children are very challenging: often from difficult backgrounds with difficult attitudes; influenced by a world that often instills troubling values. But if you can break through with just one or two a year – and other teachers can do the same – all of a sudden you are transforming multiple lives.

Well practice: creating a 'ripple effect'

- **Start small. Try and make one connection each half-term to start with. That would still be six a year.**
- **Look for the positives and name them: 'You ask great questions. That's a real strength.'**
- **Be considered and intentional in your daily actions: tone, body language, availability**
- **Create your 'ripple folder': Somewhere you can record small wins, thank-you notes, and moments of connection – like another teacher, Pete: 'I've got a book at work, which has got all the really special letters and cards and those kinds of things.'**

Lao Tzu's oft quoted: 'A journey of a thousand miles begins with a single step,' (6th century BCE) reminds us that beginning to make a difference does not require a grand gesture. One moment can lead to another, but it is the first moment (or step) that has to happen before the rest can follow. We started off in Chapter 1 talking about the importance of teaching. This is another example. The cumulative potential for teaching to change the world is aptly demonstrated. If everyone made that connection and had that belief in one young person a year, and that was transformative in that child's life, it would not be long at all before individual transformation became group transformation, and in turn became *societal* transformation.

James Kerr discusses another idea from the All Blacks: '...leave the jersey in a better place' (Kerr, 2013, p.14). This idea proposes that each player should work on incremental improvements that helps to move forward their role and the team. The same mindset can be incredibly helpful for teaching. What can you do to help that child develop? What can you contribute in your school to move Design Technology forward? How can Year 4 be better by the end of this year than it was at the start? If you can 'leave the jersey in a better place', you will not only be impacting in the moment. Your actions will ripple out through lives and communities over time.

The 'ripple effect' in practice

This idea draws on much of what we have already looked at through the course of this book.

In Chapter 1, we looked at, 'the spark': why you get into teaching in the first place. We examined practical ways to hold onto this passion.

In Chapter 2, we discussed joy, hope and positivity, and Chapter 3 unpicked the centrality of relationships.

As teachers, we are continually modelling. Yes, when we're writing or solving equations but, arguably more importantly, when we are being humans. The excitement (or lack of) we bring to the classroom; our attitudes to work, learning, other people, the world around us; and the relationships we forge, how we forge them and how we tend to them. All of these provide models for the young people we work with. They are continually watching and learning from each decision and each interaction. One teacher I spoke to, Fozia said: 'I want students to come in saying, "This is why I'm doing this." If they understand the why, they'll thrive. And it's all about building that trust.'

♥ Well moment ♥

What are you modelling today?

- How you handle mistakes?
- How you talk about yourself?
- How you respond when you're frustrated?
- How you demonstrate curiosity?

The children are watching how you behave, what you say, and what you do. It may not always feel like it, but they are using this to inform their understanding of how to act in the world.

Now this is not a clarion call for perfection. Far from it. Expectations of perfection are as damaging as expectations of poor behaviour or low attainment. And trying to model perfection is a) a one way road to failure, b) deeply damaging to you and c) entirely unhelpful and unrealistic for our students. But it is about striving to be the best versions of ourselves.

This picks up on the themes from Chapters 4, 5 and 6. Here we looked at how to manage the load, how to hold onto yourself and keep growing.

Because being a teacher is about being a human first and foremost. If you are stressed and exhausted, you will not be the best version of yourself. Likewise, if you are consumed by the job. Only by working on yourself from the inside out; reflecting, growing and developing, can you become an ever better version of yourself. Not perfect. Not flawless. You in all your deeply flawed, deeply complex glory: growing, learning, caring deeply, trying to understand, connecting. That is what it means to be human. That is where you can make the greatest difference.

Setting the weather

'You set the weather in your classroom.' It's a great truism I've noticed both in the classroom and with my own children. If I am stressed, they are more irritable. If I am manic, they are bouncing off the walls. If I'm calm, so are they. If I am positive and focused on solutions… you guessed it.

The people around us respond to how we show up. For children in particular, this is not just in the moment. How we deal with conflict, learning, challenges, humour and resilience all impacts children's views and approaches.

Attachment Theory was first described in John Bowlby's 1969 book, *Attachment and Loss*. It was later expanded upon by Mary Ainsworth, particularly her *Strange Situation* study. This provided the first empirical evidence to support Bowlby's initial work (Ainsworth and Blehar, 1978).

Attachment Theory will be familiar to many of you. It describes how our earliest relationships with our caregivers shape our future relationships, behaviours and emotional development. Ainsworth's study gave us four categories:

- **Secure attachment:** Children feel confident in their caregivers due to their responsiveness and availability (physically and emotionally). As a result, they are able to explore, be curious, take risks and build healthy relationships.
- **Anxious attachment:** Children have a high need for reassurance and comfort from their caregivers. They are overly concerned with what other people think and how they might react. As a result, they are fearful, less able to explore the world around them and can be overly demanding of attention in relationships.
- **Avoidant attachment:** Children are disconnected from their caregivers. They struggle to connect and can be emotionally 'cold'. In these instances,

people can be distant, unable to share emotionally and 'open up'. They can struggle to understand people who are more emotionally open and can find building closeness with others a challenge.

- **Disorganised attachment:** Children who have been abused, neglected or experienced trauma can often demonstrate disorganised attachment. Here there is both a need for emotional attachment and reassurance alongside a fearfulness of rejection. This can lead to contradictory behaviours and a disconnection from or anxiety about relationships.

Whilst this theory focuses on our relationship with our primary caregiver (for most of us our parents), it also applies to secondary caregivers such as teachers. Our ability to connect and how we model social behaviours all directly impact upon how children grow and develop.

Impacting on culture

Beyond the classroom, we also have the power to impact on colleagues and the overall culture of the school. Another of James Kerr's lessons from the All Blacks was, 'no dickheads'. The idea that: 'No one is bigger than the team and individual brilliance does not automatically lead to outstanding results. One selfish mindset will infect a collective culture' (Kerr, 2013, p.81).

To reframe that more neutrally: how you show up impacts on everyone around you.

Well practice: starting the day well

Imagine yourself as a bottle of cola.

- Wake-up, think, 'what an awful night's sleep': shake the bottle.
- Stub your toe on the side of the bed, think, 'why do these things always happen to me?': shake the bottle.
- Out of milk, 'life's not fair!': shake the bottle.
- Traffic, 'typical!': shake the bottle.

You get to work, you are ready to explode and the day hasn't started.

Starting the day with a positive mantra can help:

- Today I am going to be positive and happy.
- I am capable of achieving great things.
- I embrace challenges as opportunities for growth.

Culture is often described as 'how we do things around here'. The idea that it is everyone's collective behaviours, actions and decisions that ultimately create an organisational culture. Often, you can feel powerless within an organisation. But you can make choices about how you show up each day and, through these choices, begin to influence others. If more people start showing up differently, before you know it, 'how you do things around here' has started to change as a result.

Don't get me wrong, just smiling and saying good morning to colleagues is not about to transform a toxic culture built upon power dynamics, fear and bullying. However, just as we have explored with the children, small actions can have a significant impact.

♥ Well moment ♥

- Smiling and saying good morning may not be transformative overnight but it's a good start.
- Find solutions: be a '2 per cent-er' (Cope and Whittaker, 2012) – the sort of person who has a can-do attitude. Photocopier not working, how can you help?
- Communicate: share concerns openly rather than sowing discontent and becoming a well poisoner. You feel the planning format isn't working? Speak to someone about why you think that is and how you think it could be improved.

Create your tidal wave of transformation

The Butterfly Effect was first expounded by Edward Lorenz (1972), a meteorologist and mathematician. This theory gained real traction in the seventies and eighties as Chaos Theory began to expand.

Lorenz's thinking stemmed from weather simulations he was running. He'd rounded one of the variables to three decimal places rather than six. This one small change led to a drastic alteration in the weather predictions over the following two months. His visualisation – that a butterfly flapping its wings in one part of the world could eventually lead to a tidal wave somewhere else entirely – has become embedded in popular culture.

For our purposes, the overarching idea – that we operate in complex systems and so small changes can make huge differences – is important. It may feel like you are a butterfly and can make little difference no matter how hard you flap. But it might be that your choice to be open and curious about a colleague's behaviour could set off a whole chain of events that are the basis of a much greater change. And even if that isn't the case, you'll feel better for having tried. As Lucy, a secondary school teacher, said: 'It's those little things – a message from a parent, a student remembering something years later. That's what tells you it mattered. That's the work.'

♥ Well moment ♥

Be a butterfly

Find a child you have not connected with yet. Make time to get to know them. Sit next to them in class. Spend some time with them at break or lunchtime. Chat to them on a trip. Find out what it is they like, what they're interested in, what motivates them. Really see them. No judgement, no agenda. Just make the time to really connect on a human level.

Who knows, maybe that will be the moment that ripples out through their lifetime and the lifetimes of everyone they impact on.

Believing in the process

So much of this work is invisible. It's why the heroic teacher narrative is so compelling. In this, you see your impact in the moment of revelation or the child expressing the impact you've had on their lives. But most of your impact is unseen; below the surface. Maybe (very occasionally) you'll bump into a child you taught and they'll tell you that it was your drama lessons that transformed their confidence and took them from a nervous, trembling loner to a confident business tycoon ('oh, and here's a donation of one million for the school, by the way'). Or a colleague you challenged in a meeting will tell you it was this that prompted them to reflect, invest in some coaching, and completely change their approach to work and life. For the vast majority of the time though, you won't know. And neither will they.

The fallibility of memory

It's easy to attribute and make links between where we are now and what impacted on this. However, memory is deeply flawed. How we remember and interpret events changes over time and space. It is not passive (like opening a file on a computer) but active: we are reconstructing the events. This means that each time there is room for it to change based on our current perspectives, environment, stimuli etc.

Elizabeth Loftus' (1974) work on 'the misinformation effect' showed that multiple factors changed people's memories of events. In one experiment, she showed people videos of car crashes and then asked them to estimate the speed of the car, changing the key verb each time: crashed, hit, bumped. The verb correlated to the speed estimates. So 'crashed' mapped to a faster estimated speed than 'bumped' (Loftus and Palmer, 1974).

It is wonderful to imagine that someone, someday will link your effort and sacrifice to their positive outcomes. However, you might need to accept that won't happen often.

If it looks like a duck, swims like a duck, and quacks like a duck, then it probably is a duck

The fact is, if you turn up as an emotionally available, energised, positive, connected, joyful human being as often as you can, you are going to make those differences. There is a leap of faith needed, but you all make those every day. By investing in and taking care of yourself, you can turn up for the children and your colleagues. If you do this regularly, you will make a difference. This difference will resonate far beyond your classroom and your school. You will be part of something far greater than yourself that positively impacts individuals, families, communities and societies.

The legacy builders

When it comes down to it, teaching is so much more than a job. It is a force. A force for change. A force for improvement. A force for good. A force that can change lives and also change the world we live in. Finding a way to step back from the day-to-day and see this can help your wellbeing because it connects you back to your spark and your purpose. Does it negate the challenges of *that* difficult class on a cold Tuesday morning when the whiteboard isn't working and your line manager is coming in to observe you and, frankly, you feel they've got it in for you? Only you can truly answer that. My hope is that it does help, a bit. At that moment, you can't change the fact you're about to teach *that* class, or the weather, date, IT or what other people choose to do or how they choose to behave. However, I hope that by following some of the advice in this chapter and the book as a whole – reconnecting with what matters most; finding the joy; drawing on your relationships etc. – can help you to shift your mindset because this is somewhere you always have agency.

Stories from the classroom

'This is why I do this job'

Kristy vividly remembers bumping into one of her very first pupils years later. The girl had been eager in Kristy's Year 6 English class, voraciously borrowing Shakespeare books despite a difficult home life. Kristy lost touch as the girl moved on, but suddenly here she was, grown up and beaming. She excitedly told Kristy that she was headed to college – something no one in her family had done – and had earned incredible GCSEs. 'Miss, I got all 8s and 9s,' she said, modest about her grades. Kristy nearly laughed and gave her a hug: 'You are amazing,' she insisted. In that moment Kristy's pride was overwhelming. It hit her that in a tough school where many kids beat the odds daily, this girl had persisted and succeeded. 'They defy odds every day. This is why I do this job,' Kristy thought as they parted. Encounters like this, seeing former students thriving, remind her that every late night and extra effort was worth it.

Kristy, primary school teacher

Handing on the mantle

Pete was asked to carry out an observation of a teacher in his Trust recently. He told me: 'I went into the classroom and I had no idea that I'd taught her GCSE English.' What followed was one of the most heartfelt thank-yous Pete had ever received. The student - once labelled difficult, explained that something Pete had said in passing changed how she saw herself. Now an adult, she wanted Pete to know it mattered. Pete has a folder of messages like this: thank-you notes, letters, emails from past pupils and parents. On tough days, he opens it. 'You don't always get to see the outcomes,' he said, 'but sometimes, they find you.'

Pete, secondary school teacher

A message five years later

Fozia received an email from a former student she barely remembered. He'd been quiet and never caused trouble – easy to overlook. The message said, 'You made me believe I could go to uni. I never forgot that.' Fozia was stunned. 'I didn't even realise I'd said anything that big,' she admitted. But it reminded her that impact isn't always loud or visible. 'We say things in passing that stick,' she said. 'That's the ripple.' That one message re-anchored her in the work. 'It's why we do this – not for the thanks, but because we know it matters.'

Fozia, secondary school teacher

Well reflections

- Who can you connect with today? How will this connection add value to your day?
- What do you need to work on so you are more emotionally available?
- How will you leave the jersey in a better place by the end of this term?

Reimagining the role

9 Loving the job again (and again)

'Passion is momentary; love is enduring.'

(John Wooden, 2000)

Do you believe in love at first sight?

That cinematic moment, when the feeling overcomes you, the music strikes up (in your head of course IRL), and you fall head-over-heels. Think Jack seeing Rose for the first time as she gracefully promenades to the front of the Titanic – transfixed, James Horner's score swelling in the background, they lock eyes – love!

Now I've got you swooning with passion and ardour, allow me to dismantle it. There is no 'love at first sight'. Attraction? sure. But love is deep and meaningful; built on shared experiences and overcoming challenges. It requires a knowledge that is far, far beyond the superficial. Sure it's tempting – and positively thrust upon us by popular culture – to tell the story of when you first saw each other across a crowded room and knew they were 'the one'. But history is written by the winners. And in this case, that's the relationships that endured.

Once you've built true love through hard work, sacrifice, compromise and empathy, it's easy – almost expected – to tell the story of how it all began as a Titanic, Rose and Jack-esque, cinematic moment. And if you did lock eyes and think that's the one, then built the relationship, it turns out it was true! But in that first moment, it was not love. (You can tell I'm a hoot on Valentine's Day!)

The point of all this is to show that teaching is not something you love every day, every week, every year. As we saw in our first chapter, so many people come into the profession filled with energy, excitement and a real spark. But, like any relationship, that initial spark fades. And that's not a bad thing. Relationships – whether with people or careers – have to follow a path. We start off filled with energy and excitement, but that is not sustainable. Over time we become more comfortable. Maybe there are things that annoy or frustrate us. But there are also bits that we love deeply. We have times when we lose our way and it's hard. Over time we create a real, enduring love. One that is deep and meaningful and connected.

The whole point of this is that it isn't a quick fix. It's not about just 'doing' something - or even a list of somethings - and, voila, enduring love. It's about showing up, investing in the elements we've covered in this book, and knowing that teaching has all the component parts for a life well-lived. It's about taking the rough with the smooth. There are challenges, but those are part of what makes it worthwhile.

My love story

Chloe and I are everything to each other. We connected and fell hard. It was exciting and beautiful. We're both strong personalities and, after the initial rush, we wrestled for control in the relationship. Slowly we found our way: created shared norms, identified roles, and improved communication. It became calmer and our love for each other grew as we grew together. Then Eva was born. Our world was turned upside down. From only having each other to think about, suddenly there was someone else.

Adjusting to life as three was tough. Noa arrived 21 months later and 'full-on' became 'all-consuming'. This also coincided with me taking on the Headship at Kensington Primary School.

The 12 years since then have seen many iterations.

We've now been together for over 20 years and they've been the happiest 20 years of my life. So many magical memories. It's also been tough at times. It's taken a lot of hard work. There are times when it hasn't been great. Even times when we could have walked away. But we didn't. We stuck with it. Because we knew it was something worth fighting for. And through that effort and those challenges, we built something of true value and meaning. Something that sustains us both. That is the central part of our lives: our joy, our hope and positivity, and our wellbeing.

That is love. Forged in the fires, not glanced across a room.

Putting in the hard yards

The same applies to all aspects of our lives. Creating true meaning and worth takes determination. Nothing of value is achieved without hard work. Can you find easier jobs than teaching? Yes! But does that make them better or more fulfilling? Not necessarily. Will there be times you can't stand teaching and you've had enough? Absolutely. Yesterday for example: most of SLT were out; I had back-to-back meetings; and fifteen minutes before lunch I got a message to say that a crow and two pigeons had flown into the dinner hall. I was also picking up a couple of challenging HR issues, a safeguarding situation, and an ongoing union discussion. I juggled shooing pigeons out of the hall whilst going over how to deal with these issues. By 6.00 pm, I'd had it.

Of course, I'm not advocating sticking it out regardless. Teaching isn't for everyone and it doesn't work at every life stage for every person. For some people, there will be a point where the right call is to walk away.

I've wanted to walk away many times. When I talk to friends about their 'work' I sometimes don't know whether to laugh or cry. If I go to a training course in Central London and see people sat drinking a coffee at 9.30 am in Starbucks, when I've already been in school for two hours before dashing across town, I can't quite understand where it all went so wrong. But here's the kicker, with the exception of my fellow teachers, I don't know anyone who loves what they do as much as me.

Wellbeing is not about doing less or making things easier. True wellbeing comes from meaning, purpose and connection. From facing up to challenges, overcoming them and growing as a result. From finding the strategies that work for you and help you to feel lighter, focus on the positives, and hold onto the good memories. From working hard at something and achieving. From making a real, tangible difference.

That is what love is. It is not a constant. It goes through stages. We can fall out of love. But we can also fall back in. True love is enduring and deep. It takes a lot of time. But if you can build that, it is transformative in every aspect of your life.

Well practice: love the job again challenge

Your one-week, 'love the job again' challenge. This week, I want you to have:

- one moment of genuine joy with students
- one boundary you commit to
- one colleague you chat with
- one thing you let go of.

Note them down. Return to them. Or repeat this next half-term and see what's changed.

Why we fall out of love

There are many reasons why people can fall out of love with a job. Just like relationships, this can happen in a one-off moment but, more often than not, it is a cumulative drift that happens over time. But in almost every case, it's recoverable, if you seek out the support and relevant strategies to help you navigate the moments where you feel a drift. The strategies and guidance in this book provide you with a template that will help, if you want it to.

Let's also be clear: some of the reasons people fall out of love with teaching are structural, systemic and entirely outside their control. A toxic school culture, poor leadership, or government policy can make even the best teachers feel disempowered, disincentivised and demotivated. I don't want to ignore that or pretend there's a magic fix. But I do want to offer a different kind of power, the kind that comes from choosing your response, when and where you can.

Wear and tear

What are some of the circumstances that may start to impact your love of teaching?

Say you've got a challenging class. You like a challenge. You find solutions. You have some successes. But, day-after-day, you're coming up against the same issues. It starts to eat your time and sap your will. Then you're asked to support another teacher. They don't really want your help. Your relationship gets difficult. And no one has said thank you. Or recognised it.

I could keep layering this up. The point is, sometimes the weight of this all becomes too much. The missed lunchtimes, the late nights, the seemingly pointless tasks. One day, you simply realise you're no longer in love. The spark has gone. The purpose is lost. You're just unhappy and doing a job and, ultimately, that's not what you signed up for or what you want out of your working life.

Not with a whimper but with a bang

Just as in relationships, sometimes it is one big event that will break your trust and love. Or it might just be that your world changes. A toxic culture, an incident with a senior leader, a broken promise, a change in circumstances. Sometimes it comes to an end suddenly.

'I'm bored!'

Not something we want to hear from our pupils and certainly not something we want to feel in our jobs. But sometimes, people do get bored. Same curriculum; same lessons; same challenges, year-in, year-out, it can end up feeling like Groundhog Day. There's nothing worse than feeling like you are stuck on that hamster wheel and can't escape.

Losing yourself

In Chapter 5 we explored this in great depth. The job can be great for all the right reasons, but many of those reasons can also consume us if we are not careful. When does caring for the children become not caring for your own family or friends? And when does it become not caring for yourself?

What brings people back

Just like any relationship, sometimes the best decision is to move on. Not every love story is written in the stars. The same applies to jobs. For some, this may mean deciding to leave teaching. For others, they just need a break. Others may need a change in role. In teaching, a change in school is often the spark that reignites people's love. School cultures vary hugely. It is an enormous benefit of the profession that you can move to a different school and find a culture that better fits your current situation.

What can reconnect us to the job?

Reigniting the spark

We explored the initial spark in Chapter 1. Rediscovering your 'why' can help remind you what first got you into teaching. Some of the above reasons for falling out of love can create a barrier that obscures why you got into teaching. If you feel you are not making a difference, that you are spending time on tasks that have minimal impact, that you are too stretched to deliver for your children in the way you would like. Finding ways to reconnect to this spark is key.

'Those kind of passion projects really keep me going' (Nuren, secondary school teacher who introduced AI technology into her school to help teachers reduce repetitive tasks).

In Chapter 2 we talked about 'wearing your rose-tinted spectacles' – this can be a great way to reignite that spark. In Chapter 4 we looked at workload and at, 'deciding on what matters and letting the rest burn'. Just taking time to reflect on why you got into teaching, prioritising this – relationships, inspiration, making a difference – finding ways to remove the barriers, and then focusing on your successes, can help to lift you up and start kindling that flame again.

The power of relationships

In Chapter 3 we looked at the fundamental importance of relationships both in life and in teaching. Often it is these relationships that can bring us back to loving the job again. A colleague who inspires you; a line manager who empowers you; a child who needs you. Following the guidance in Chapter 3, looking for opportunities to build deep, meaningful relationships, and investing time and energy into these, can help bring back your love for the job.

'I get to come in every day and teach children things that are important... it's about the impact you can have on little people's lives' (Sonya, primary school teacher).

Reclaiming your self

In Chapter 5 we looked at holding onto yourself – the importance of this and ways to do it. Sometimes teaching can feel very all or nothing. We often talk about the job being, 'a marathon not a sprint'. Are you better adjusting your expectations for what is required of you so that the job is sustainable? Or are you going all in and, ultimately, burning out? Not all aspects of this will be in your control, but what elements are? What changes can you make tomorrow that make it more sustainable? What might you choose to do 'well enough' if it helped you stay in the job longer?

'There's nothing that negatively impacts my well-being more than being bored... trying to solve those problems is hugely fulfilling' (Lucy, secondary school teacher).

Mindset

It is easy, at times, to fall into an external mindset – we looked at this in Chapter 6. Yes – some of what makes this job hard is visited upon you. Not everything is in your control. What is, is your mindset. Looking at the impact you are having now, and for the future (as explored in Chapter 8), is a great way of helping to rebuild that love. It can be easy to slip into cynicism at times, particularly when you're tired. That is human and entirely understandable. When I catch myself in this mindset, I ask: 'who is this really serving?'

'I now can't imagine doing anything different… I do love it' (Joe, primary school teacher).

Loving the job on your terms

No-one loves everything, every day. No job is perfect. It is all trade-offs. There's lots about teaching that isn't great, whether at a system, school or individual level. But this can apply to any job. And so, ultimately, it comes down to those trade-offs. Is the sense of purpose worth the challenging behaviour? Is the difference you can make worth the hours you work? Is the joy of working with children worth the constraints you face? Only you can answer those questions. And those questions (and answers) will change over time.

What is crucial is taking control of the elements you do have agency over and using that to carve out a job that works for you. That, again, will vary over time depending on your own circumstances. The teacher you were at 25 is likely to be very different to the teacher you are at 45. Growth and wisdom come with experience, and teachers can use this to adapt their skills over time. This is another reason teaching is such a great career.

Commitment to anything is active. Love is active. It takes focus, energy, and practice. It happens when we work hard, try to solve problems, and think deeply. It is not something that anyone else can do for us, nor is it a one-off event.

♥ Well moment ♥

- **Identify weekly rituals that reconnect you to your spark.**
- **Prioritise connecting with children/colleagues.**
- **Redefine what success looks like for you, now.**

I'm not saying any of this is easy. I've had days and weeks where I wanted to walk away too. And I've been part of schools that made it harder, not easier. I've also seen – and felt – the difference when we get it right. The people who inspired this book – and whose voices resonate through it – are all finding ways to make it work for them.

Loving the job again is not about a grand gesture or transformation. It is about putting into practice everything we have covered over the course of the previous eight chapters. It's knowing that this takes effort. It's accepting the fact that there will be times you fall out of love. But also knowing that, through implementing these strategies, you can find your way back to loving the job and finding purpose in the day to day.

Teaching can be hard. It can challenge us. And that can be compounded rather than alleviated by the system and school cultures and structures. But if you can find a way to make it work for you, there is no job that is more rewarding, meaningful or joyful. Teaching really is the world's most important job.

Well practice: weekly intentions for wellbeing

Set intentions for the week ahead. Try to seek out:

- one moment of genuine joy with students
- one boundary you commit to and honour
- one colleague you connect with
- one thing you let go of.

Note them down. Return to them. Or repeat this next half-term and see what's changed.

Stories from the classroom

Recommitting after a toxic experience

Jodie nearly fell out of love with teaching early in her career. Working in a school with chronically poor student behaviour left her overwhelmed and disillusioned. She didn't feel she got the support she needed. Eventually, Jodie made the difficult decision to leave that school.

She left that job expecting that constant chaos was unavoidable in teaching. Instead of quitting the profession outright however, Jodie made a quiet choice to try again in a different environment. She joined a new school with a more supportive culture. The change was transformative. In her new role, Jodie found she could actually enjoy teaching again. The contrast was stark: with better systems and support, she no longer took stress home each day. As she put it, 'my head space is at school, it's left there,' instead of haunting her evenings and weekends. Now Jodie speaks with a sense of purpose and relief. She's 'happy to come back' to work, having rediscovered the joy of the classroom. Jodie's story illustrates a quiet recommitment. Rather than giving up on teaching after struggle, she sought out a place where she could love the job again, proving that sometimes a change of setting can revive one's passion.

Jodie, secondary school teacher

Back from burnout

For Kristy, loving the job again came after a period of profound personal and professional struggle. By her account, 'the last two years have just been a bit much,' a buildup of stress that pushed her toward a breaking point.

Kristy found herself on the verge of burnout or even leaving. What pulled her back was not a grand epiphany, but the steady presence of colleagues and a school community that refused to let her fail. She told me that 'if it wasn't for these people at the school *dragging* me back' she does not think she'd still be in teaching today.

By opening up and sharing her struggles, Kristy allowed others to help her rediscover her confidence. Over time, their encouragement rekindled her sense of purpose. In fact, when she faced personal tragedy she realised 'I need to be at work, because it just kept me going'.

Teaching, with all its challenges, became her anchor through hardship. Kristy's case shows a nuanced, unsentimental truth: after nearly burning out, it was the quiet support of trusted colleagues and the routine of the classroom that helped her regain her love for the job. Her recommitment wasn't flashy; it was a gradual healing that allowed her passion to return and endure.

Kristy, primary school teacher

Sustaining joy by embracing highs and lows

Francesca, a veteran secondary school teacher, demonstrates how to love the job over decades without becoming jaded. After nearly twenty years in the classroom, she remains enthusiastic, but she admits that teaching is never perfect. She draws inspiration from an even more experienced colleague who taught for over 30 years and 'was still incredibly passionate' about the work. Seeing someone teach with such joy 'gives me hope and pride in the profession,' Francesca told me.

Her secret to longevity: accept the hard days along with the good. 'You're going to moan, you're going to have bad days, but you're only human, and I think it's really important to realise that.'

Instead of idealising the job, Francesca acknowledges the struggles as part of it. This grounded outlook allows her to relish the quiet victories – the 'little moments that just make you think, wow, what I'm doing is making a difference.' Whether it's a formerly struggling pupil's success or a heartfelt thank you from a parent, Francesca lets those moments rekindle her purpose whenever it flickers. By embracing change, finding meaning in small victories, and forgiving herself for the tough days, she continually rediscovers why she loves teaching – again and again.

Francesca, secondary school teacher

Well reflections

- What do you love most about the job?
- If you've had a difficult time, what was it that helped you reconnect?
- What does loving the job look like now, in this season of your career?
- What's one thing in your control that you could change that would shape your job into one that you love again?
- Have your needs or values shifted since you started teaching (or since you started reading this book?)

References

Ackerman, D. (1991) *A Natural History of the Senses.* New York: Vintage Books.

Ainsworth, M. D. S., Blehar, M. C., Waters, E. and Wall, S. (1978) *Patterns of Attachment: A Psychological Study of the Strange Situation*. Hillsdale, NJ: Lawrence Erlbaum Associates.

Alqurashi, F. (2023) 'Impact of Chronic Stress on Learning and Memory in Students: A Review of Recent Literature', Cureus, 15(5).

Bargh, J. A., Chen, M. and Burrows, L. (1996) 'Automaticity of Social Behavior: Direct Effects of Trait Construct and Stereotype Activation on Action', Journal of Personality and Social Psychology, 71(2), pp. 230–244

BBC Worklife (2021) *The damaging effects of 'boreout' at work.* [Online] Available at: https://www.bbc.com/worklife/article/20210701-the-damaging-effects-of-boreout-at-work

Bethune, A. (2018) *Wellbeing in the Primary Classroom: A practical guide to teaching happiness.* London: Bloomsbury Education.

Bowlby, J. (1969) *Attachment and Loss: Vol. 1. Attachment.* London: Hogarth Press.

Baband, E. Y., Inbar, J. and Rosenthal, R. (1982) 'Pygmalion, Galatea, and the Golem: Investigations of Biased and Unbiased Teachers', Journal of Educational Psychology, 74(4), pp.459–474.

Bretherton, I. (1992) 'The origins of attachment theory: John Bowlby and Mary Ainsworth', Developmental Psychology, 28(5), pp.759–775.

Brophy, J. E. (1983) *Teacher Expectations and Student Achievement.* New York: Longman.

Brown, B. (2015) *Daring Greatly: How the Courage to Be Vulnerable Transforms the Way We Live, Love, Parent, and Lead.* London: Penguin Life.

Burkeman, O. (2022) *Four Thousand Weeks: Time and How to Use It.* London: Vintage.

Cain, S. (2012) *Quiet: The power of introverts in a world that can't stop talking.* London: Penguin.

Clear, J. (2018) *Atomic Habits: An Easy and Proven Way to Build Good Habits and Break Bad Ones.* London: Random House.

Cope, A. and Whittaker, A. (2012) *The Art of Being Brilliant: Transform Your Life by Doing What Works for You.* Chichester: Capstone Publishing.

Csikszentmihalyi, M. (1990) *Flow: The psychology of optimal experience.* New York: Harper & Row.

Conway, M. A., & Pleydell-Pearce, C. W. (2000). 'The Construction of Autobiographical Memories in the Self-Memory System', Psychological Review, 107(2), pp.261–288.

Cowell, C. (2018) 'Cressida Cowell: 'Miss Mellows just let me write'. *TES Magazine.* [Online] Available from: https://www.tes.com/magazine/archive/cressida-cowell-miss-mellows-just-let-me-write (Accessed 15 November 2025)

Department for Education, Get into Teaching – Every Lesson Shapes a Life (2023) UK Government [Television Advert].

Desert Island Discs, Ian Wright, former footballer and broadcaster. 2020. BBC Radio 4. 16 Feb, 11:15

Dix, P (2017) *When the Adults Change, Everything Changes: Seismic shifts in school behaviour.* Carmarthen: Independent Thinking Press.

Dweck, C. S. (2006) *Mindset: The New Psychology of Success.* New York: Random House.

Eastwood, O. (2022) *Belonging.* London: Quercus.

Education Endowment Foundation. (2025) Teaching and Learning Toolkit. Available at: https://educationendowmentfoundation.org.uk/education-evidence/teaching-learning-toolkit (Accessed 15 November 2025)

Education Support (2024) Teacher wellbeing index 2024. London: Education Support. Available at: https://www.educationsupport.org.uk/media/ftwl04cs/twix-2024.pdf (Accessed: 27 June 2025).

Ellis, S., Tupper, H. (2020) Amazing If *About.* Available at: https://www.amazingif.com/about/

Emerald, D. (2005) *The Power of TED: The Empowerment Dynamic.* Bainbridge Island, WA: Polaris Publishing.

Fennell, A. (2025) *Career change statistics UK.* StandOut CV. Available at: https://standout-cv.com/stats/career-change-statistics-uk

Fredrickson, B. L. (2011) *Positivity: Groundbreaking Research to Release Your Inner Optimist and Thrive.* London: Oneworld Publications.

Fussman, C., 2010. What I've Learned: John Wooden Esquire. Available at: https://www.esquire.com/sports/interviews/a1900/learned-john-wood-0200/ (Accessed 15th November 2025)

Future Learn (2022) *The Future of Learning.* Available at: https://www.futurelearn.com/info/thefutureoflearning

Gallup (2025) The Q12®: The World's Leading Employee Engagement Survey. Available at: https://www.gallup.com/q12-employee-engagement-survey/ (Accessed: 26 September 2025).

Haig, M. (2021) *The Comfort Book.* Edinburgh: Canongate.

Harvard Second Generation Study (2015) Harvard Second Generation Study. Available at: https://www.adultdevelopmentstudy.org/ (Accessed 15 November 2025)

Hattie, J. (2009) *Visible Learning: A synthesis of over 800 meta-analyses relating to achievement.* Abingdon: Routledge.

Henrich, J. (2017) *The secret of our success: how culture is driving human evolution, domesticating our species, and making us smarter.* 2nd printing, 1st paperback edn. Princeton, NJ: Princeton University Press.

Hitt, C. (2019) Hidden heroines: Could Betty Campbell win statue vote?. Available at https://www.bbc.co.uk/news/uk-wales-46508398 (Accessed 13 November 2025)

Jordan, M. (2008). Failure. [Video]. Nike. Available at: https://www.youtube.com/watch?v=GuXZFQKKF7A [Accessed 7 Oct. 2025]

Karpman, S. B. (1968) 'Fairy Tales and Script Drama Analysis', Transactional Analysis Bulletin, 7(26), pp. 39–43.

Kerr, J. (2013) *Legacy: What the All Blacks Can Teach Us About the Business of Life.* London: Constable.

King, M. L. 1960. *"Keep Moving from This Mountain," Address at Spelman College on 10 April 1960.* [Online]. Available from: https://kinginstitute.stanford.edu/king-papers/documents/keep-moving-mountain-address-spelman-college-10-april-1960 (Accessed 17 November 2025)

Lao Tzu (1963) *Tao Te Ching*. Translated by D.C. Lau. London: Penguin Classics.

Legend, J. (2017) 'By Empowering Teachers, We Can Level The Playing Field For Every Student'. *HuffPost.* [Online]. Available from: https://www.huffpost.com/entry/level-playing-field-for-students_b_59ff571fe4b0baea26328d51 (Accessed 15 November 2025)

Loftus, E. F. and Palmer, J. C. (1974) 'Reconstruction of Automobile Destruction: An Example of the Interaction Between Language and Memory', Journal of Verbal Learning and Verbal Behavior 13(5), pp.585–589

Lorenz, E.N. (1972) 'Predictability: Does the Flap of a Butterfly's Wings in Brazil Set Off a Tornado in Texas?' Paper presented at the American Association for the Advancement of Science, Washington, D.C., 29 December 1972. Available at: https://eapsweb.mit.edu/sites/default/files/Butterfly_1972.pdf (Accessed: 18 July 2025).

Lysova, E. I., Allan, B. A., Dik, B. J., Duffy, R. D. and Steger, M. F. (2019) 'Fostering meaningful work in organizations: A review and research agenda', Journal of Vocational Behavior, 110, pp.374–389. Available at: https://doi.org/10.1016/j.jvb.2018.07.004 (Accessed 15 November 2025)

Magness, S. (2022) *Do Hard Things: Why We Get Resilience Wrong and the Surprising Science of Real Toughness*. First edn. New York: HarperCollins.

Manyika, J., Lund, S., Chui, M., Bughin, J., Woetzel, L., Batra, P., Ko, R. & Sanghvi, S. (2017) *Jobs lost, jobs gained: What the future of work will mean for jobs, skills, and wages.* McKinsey Global Institute. Available at: https://www.mckinsey.com/featured-insights/future-of-work/jobs-lost-jobs-gained-what-the-future-of-work-will-mean-for-jobs-skills-and-wages

Martin, K. (2012) *The Outstanding Organization: Generate Business Results by Eliminating Chaos and Building the Foundation for Everyday Excellence.* Columbus, Ohio: McGraw Hill.

McGaugh, J. L. (2003) *Memory and Emotion: The Making of Lasting Memories*. New York: Columbia University Press.

Montaigne, M. (1877) *The Complete Essays of Montaigne.* Translated by Charles Cotton, rev. William Carew Hazlitt. London: Cassell & Co.

Monty Python (1974) 'The Four Yorkshiremen', Monty Python Live at Drury Lane [Vinyl]. London: Charisma Records.

Niebuhr, R. (1986) *The Essential Reinhold Niebuhr: Selected Essays and Addresses.* McAfee Brown, R. ed. New Haven, Connecticut: Yale University Press.

NHS (2022) 5 steps to mental wellbeing. Available at: https://www.nhs.uk/mental-health/self-help/guides-tools-and-activities/five-steps-to-mental-wellbeing/ (Accessed 15 November 2025)

People Management (2021) *Two-thirds of workers taking multiple jobs, study finds.* Available at: https://www.peoplemanagement.co.uk/article/1743090/two-thirds-workers-taking-multiple-jobs-study-finds

Phillipson, B. 2024. *Bridget Phillipson's speech at the Confederation of School Trusts (CST) Conference.* [Online} Available at: https://www.gov.uk/government/speeches/bridget-phillipsons-speech-to-the-confederation-of-school-trusts (Accessed 15 November 2025)

Pine II, B. J. and Gilmore, J. H. (2006) *Look: A Practical Guide for Improving Your Observational Skills.* San Francisco: Greenleaf Book Group Press.

Pink, D. H. (2010) *Drive: The Surprising Truth About What Motivates Us.* London: Canongate.

Robinson, K and Aronica, L. (2014) *Finding Your Element: How to Discover Your Talents and Passions and Transform Your Life.* London: Penguin Books.

Roser, M. (2019) A short history of global living conditions and why it matters that we know it. Our World in Data. Available at: https://ourworldindata.org/extreme-poverty-in-brief (Accessed: 27 June 2025).

Rosling, H. (2019) *Factfulness: ten reasons we're wrong about the world – and why things are better than you think.* London: Sceptre.

Rozin, P. and Royzman, E.B. (2001). Negativity bias, negativity dominance, and contagion. Personality and Social Psychology Review, [online] 5(4), pp.296–320. Available at: doi:https://doi.org/10.1207/s15327957pspr0504_2.

Robertson, C.E., Pröllochs, N., Schwarzenegger, K., Pärnamets, P., Van Bavel, J.J. and Feuerriegel, S. (2023). Negativity drives online news consumption. Nature Human Behaviour, [online] 7(7), pp.1–11. Available at: doi:https://doi.org/10.1038/s41562-023-01538-4.

Rosenthal, R. and Jacobson, L. (1968) *Pygmalion in the Classroom: Teacher Expectation and Pupils' Intellectual Development.* New York: Holt, Rinehart & Winston, 1968.

Saffi, M., Franzoni, L., Nery, R., Donelli Da Silveria, A., Andrade, C., Carvalho, G. and Stein, R. (2023) 'Laughter therapy cardiac rehabilitation in patients with stable coronary artery disease: a randomized clinical trial', European Heart Journal, 44(2). Available at: https://academic.oup.com/eurheartj/article/44/Supplement_2/ehad655.2593/7391010 (Accessed 12 November 2025)

Seligman, M. E. P. (2011) *Flourish: A New Understanding of Happiness and Wellbeing – and How to Achieve Them.* (London: Nicholas Brealey Publishing.

Seneca, L. (2018). *On the Shortness of Life.* CreateSpace Independent.

TEACH. 2022. *Oprah Winfrey Reflects on Her Favorite Teacher.* [Online]. Available from: https://www.youtube.com/watch?v=PKmEVNpxGCY (Accessed 15 November 2025)

Waldinger, R. (2015) *What makes a good life? Lessons from the longest study on happiness*. TED. Available at: https://www.ted.com/talks/robert_waldinger_what_makes_a_good_life_lessons_from_the_longest_study_on_happiness (Accessed: 26 September 2025).

Waldinger, R. J. and Schulz, M. (2025) *The Good Life: Lessons from the World's Longest Scientific Study of Happiness*. London: Rider.

Weir, P. (dir.) (1989) Dead Poets Society. [Film] Touchstone Pictures.

Whitman, W. (1959) *Complete Poetry and Selected Prose.* Miller Jr., J. E. ed. Boston: Houghton Mifflin.

Winfrey, O. (2023) 'Oprah on the Power of Teachers'. Oprah Daily. [Online]. Available from: https://www.oprahdaily.com/life/a45736808/oprah-intention-teachers/ (Accessed 15 November 2025)

World Health Organization (2024) International classification of diseases, 11th revision (ICD-11). Available at: https://icd.who.int/browse/2025-01/mms/en#129180281 (Accessed: 27 June 2025).

Zeigarnik, B. 1938. On Finished and Unfinished Tasks. In: Ellis, W. D. ed. *A Source Book Of Gestalt Psychology.* London: Routledge and Kegan Paul Ltd., pp.300–314.

Index